Trip to London

Vincenzo, Andrea, and Pietro Berghella

Copyright Page

From the same author:

- **Obstetric Evidence Based Guidelines.** Informa Healthcare, London, UK, and New York, USA (2007) [English]

- **Maternal Fetal Evidence Based Guidelines.** Informa Healthcare, London, UK, and New York, USA (2007) [English]

- **Laughter, the best medicine. Jokes for everyone.** (2007) [English]

- **Ridere, la migliore medicina. Barzellette per bambini.** (2007) [Italiano]

- **My favorite quotes.** (2009) [English]

- **In medio stat virtus – Citazioni d'autore.** (2009) [Italiano]

- **Quello che di voi vive in me.** (2009) [Italiano]

- **Dall'altra parte dell'oceano.** (2009) [Italiano] [Translated in: **On the other side of the ocean.** (2013) [English]

- **Preterm Birth: Prevention and Management.** Wiley-Blackwell. Oxford, United Kingdom. (2010) [English]

- **From father to son.** (2010) [English]

- **Sollazzi.** (2010) [Italiano]

- **The land of religions.** (2011) [English] [Translated in: **La terra delle religioni.** (2013) [Italiano]

- **Giramondo.** (2011) [Italiano]

- **Obstetric Evidence Based Guidelines.** Informa Healthcare, London, UK, and New York, USA (2012; Second Edition) [English]

- **Maternal Fetal Evidence Based Guidelines.** Informa Healthcare, London, UK, and New York, USA (2012; Second Edition) [English]

- **Trip to London.** (2012) [English]

- **Il primo amore non si scorda mai.** (2012) [Italiano]

- **Maldives.** (2013) [English]

- **Russia.** (2013) [English]

- **Happiness: the scientific path to achieving well-being** (2014) [English]

The world is a book:
those who do not travel read only one page

Trip to London, United Kingdom
October 2011

Preparations
On March 8, 2010, I received the invitation from Roy Farquharson to be the main speaker at a conference in London. Roy is an esteemed obstetrician and gynecologist originally from Scotland, who now practices in Liverpool, England. I've met him before, in particular when the Gynaecological Club of Great Britain and Ireland visited our Department of Ob-Gyn at Thomas Jefferson University in November 2009.

The topic in medicine for which I'm better known is preterm birth. I've studied and published on its prediction with transvaginal ultrasound cervical length, and its prevention with cervical cerclage. In fact, the conference that Roy was organizing was called 'Early pregnancy cerclage.' In his email, Roy was nice enough to let me decide a date towards the end of October / beginning of November 2011. What a privilege.

Given my European background, I've always loved interacting and collaborating with my counterparts on the right side of the Atlantic. I've now lived most of my life in the United States, and have been to more than a hundred medical conferences on this left side of the Atlantic. I've attended one US annual conference, by the Society for Maternal-Fetal Medicine, for 18 years in a row. So I'm familiar with who is who, and what they are going to say, most of the time, in North America.

Roy was inviting me on behalf of the Royal College of Obstetricians and Gynecologists (RCOG), which is certainly one the most prestigious ob-gyn societies in the world. I was flattered. Given this great chance, I immediately thought about combining this meeting with a visit to the British Journal of Obstetricians and Gynecologists (BJOG). BJOG is the third or fourth most important journal for clinical ob-gyn in the world, and I've been an Editor there since 2007.

Luckily, at BJOG they set their editorial meeting dates much ahead of time, under the forward-looking leadership of Phil Steer, editor-in-chief. As one BJOG Editorial meeting around the RCOG timing was on October 26, 2011, a Thursday, I proposed October 27, a Friday, to Roy and RCOG. They kindly accepted. I had about a year and half to prepare this trip, which I looked forward to for the rest of the time.

Part of the acceptance of any major speaking engagement is talking with my wife Paola, and hopefully convincing her to accompany me. She is, rightly, less interested in following me to US cities where she has already been for meetings, and shuns away from the meetings where I'm going for too short a time, or where I'm going to be always trapped by professional duties. Otherwise, she has been a trooper in accepting to come with me for some of the international travels I've been involved with. Perhaps our best trip ever was for the FIGO (International Federation of Gynecology and Obstetrics) meeting in Kuala Lumpur, Malaysia, in 2006.

Paola and I have been to London together only once. It was for my college friend Nabil's wedding, back in 1996. We went for a weekend, which was filled with lavish and fun spousal events, and really did not allow for much site-seeing. While I've been to London a few times, ever since I was a teenager, our kids have not been there yet. At first, she resisted the thought, given the fact that Andrea and Pietro, our 13 and 11 years old sons, would miss school by going on the trip with us. But London is a fabulous place to visit, and Paola has just heard so many great things about it over time, that eventually she gave in.

Our good friends Marco and Dada Carrara have their two older kids, one studying (basic science research at the Imperial College) and the other working (engineer at British Airways) in London, and love the city. Our other friend Paolo Fortina only flies British Airways, and could be the protagonist of 'Up in the air' since he travels so much. He considers London as his favorite town in the world.

Additionally, we have several friends who actually live in London. Not just professional colleagues. My college mate Olivier de Givenchy, who I affectionately call Lolo, or even Louis XIV (Luis Quatorze), is a Frenchman who has been extremely successful as an investment banker at JP Morgan. He lives in Chelsea. I miss him a lot.

Arturo Sala is the person who introduced Paola and I. On October 29, 1993, at about 7pm, I drove him to 1208 Walnut Street, Philadelphia, where we picked Paola up at her place and went to dinner, the three of us. Two days later Paola and I were dating, and have not stopped since. He lives near the Bounds Green tube Station, in North London.

Raffaella Quieti also lives in London, in Pimlico. I've known her since we were 11 (me), 10 (her), as we both grew up in Pescara, Italy. Our sisters were best friends. Raffa (her nick name) married Charles Cartledge, originally from Belgravia, right next to Pimlico, and they have settled back here after stints in New York, Hong Kong, and Singapore. Andrea e Marta Carrara, Marco and Dada's son and daughter, live here. We may have more friends in London than in any other non-US or non-Italy town.

So the preparations for this trip spread over about 18 months. Professionally, I also collaborate with the Cochrane Library, an international organization which publishes summaries of the best medical studies. As I became an Associate Editor for them in 2011, I asked if I could visit the headquarters in Liverpool, on October 25-26, before the BJOG (on the 26) and RCOG (on the 27) other October meetings. I also contacted the Publisher of my two evidence-based medical textbooks, Robert Peden (for Informa Healthcare), who agreed to meet.

I could not wait to see again Sean Daly, my good friend and colleague from Dublin, Ireland, who was going to co-chair the RCOG Cerclage meeting. Paola, Andrea, Pietro and I had in fact been together once to the British Isles before, but on the Western Island, Ireland. In 2009 Sean had invited us for the Coombe's Hospital annual anniversary conference. The memory of that trip alone is worth remembering briefly to let you understand our connections to these two large islands of Northern Europe.

Sean was a wonderful host, and treated us like kings for five wonderful days. I'll be forever thankful to him. We arrived on a Thursday, and stayed in the heart of Dublin, at the Westbury Hotel, on Grafton Street. I had been there a few years before, again hosted by Sean, for the Coombe Hospital 175 anniversary. My professional duties went well, including lectures and grandiose black-tie events.

The touring by us four family members around Dublin and the west coast of Ireland was even better. In Dublin, we saw the book of Kells, in Trinity College, and College Green, as well as Merrion Square, St Stephen's Green, O'Connell St, and St Patrick Cathedral. But one of the highlights every time I am in Dublin is the visit to the Guinness Brewery. The kids loved the history, and the museum. Among many interesting things, they enjoyed particularly the story of how the Guinness Book of World Records came into being, basically to settle bets between wealthy Irishmen.

Sean married well, as his wife Carmen is smart, hard-working, beautiful, and gave him four good-looking children. I'd known for a long time she is from the west of Ireland, which is a region renowned for its culture and beauty. Driving their Mercedes SUV, and Austin Martin convertible, they took us on the trip west.

We visited on Saturday the unique, stunning Cliffs of Moher. Then, after lunch in a typical pub, we arrived in Galway, where Carmen is from. There we had the best time. She is one of seven children, and her extended family lives mostly there, the progeny of the local general medical doctor. On Saturday night, we felt as royals. We had dinner at Ashford Castle, one of the most beautiful castles I've ever seen.

On Sunday, while at mass, I noticed that the front pew in church was reserved for Carmen's dad and his wife, as the doctor here is still the most important figure in the community. All seven of his kids have separate huge mansions overlooking the Atlantic in the Galway countryside. The ones Sean and Carmen recently built is modern, spectacular, and you would not expect such great technology on this remote part of northern Europe. I could not wait to see them again, this time in London.

Let's get back to our current U.K. trip. After some internet work, we see that the most convenient direct flights from Philadelphia to London are not with our usual US Airways, but with British Airways. Andrea Carrara is nice enough to help us with the booking. For my 'professional' days towards the end of the trip, the RCOG books me three nights at the Domus, the bed and breakfast at their headquarters in Regent's Park. Paola as usual scans the whole web for the best accommodation for us at the beginning of the trip, from Friday to Tuesday. She books an apartment that looks right across Lambert Bridge, in Southbank, apparently in front of the House of Parliament.

In the weeks just before the trip, I begin, as usual, to write in detail what was going to happen every day, what trains to take, what sites to visit, when to meet friends, etc. I also prepare to bring with me a few of the non-medical, very personal books I've published, to give them out as gifts to friends who I was sure were going to invite us for brunches, lunches, and dinners all over London.

I think this is a nice timing for the visit. It is a personal reward for me, after having terminated the 57 chapters for the second edition of 'Maternal Fetal Evidence Based Guidelines,' with three sets of proofs reviewed, and also having handed in the 31 chapters for the second edition of 'Obstetric Evidence Based Guidelines' to Robert Peden and Informa, the Publisher. Hopefully these nine days will be a break from all the work which really was my major concern all year, January 2011 until now, October.

As I do before every major trip, I study the United Kingdom as much as my limited free time permits. I read again what I have underlined in our Fodor guide from 2002, when I last went, accompanied by my mother, as Paola could not come. I begin to read 'The secrets of London', a book in Italian written by Corrado Augias, who I know can really get you 'in the mood' for the spirit of the towns he writes about. I've already read his 'Secrets of Rome', 'Secret of Paris', and 'Secrets of New York.'

The sites to see were so many I was sure we could not see them all. I underlined as 'musts' Westminster Abbey, Big Ben and the House of Parliament, Piccadilly Circus, Trafalgar Square, and Carnaby Street. Pietro was set on visiting Madame Toussauds. If feasible, we were also interested in The City, Southbank with the Millennium Wheel, Hyde Park, Soho, East End, West End, Chelsea, Kensington, the British Museum, the Natural History Museum (with the Virgin of the Rocks), the Science Museum (with Charles Darwin), The Globe (Shakespeare's original theatre), and many other sites.

I looked carefully in the days immediately our departure for tours. Unfortunately the wonderful walking tour company that we used in Berlin was not available in London. I looked at several Double Decker bus tours. As we would arrive early in the morning, probably be jet lagged, and unsure how smooth our check-in at the rented apartment would have been, we could not agree on the time to book one. I thought 'Better this way', as sometimes you cannot over program a trip. Whatever we do in London, I'd be a first for Paola and the kids. We are stressed enough with lots of tasks at home in Philadelphia, that we can use a break here in England.

October 20, Thursday

For both Paola and I, Thursdays are the most important days of our professional week. She has 'diagnostic day', meaning the day in which she and her colleagues in the lab process all the specimens received for diagnosis of the rare metabolic diseases she is famous for. I have our weekly Maternal Fetal Medicine Clinical, Didactic, and Research meeting, in which my whole division meets. So we usually like to leave Thursday evening, making sure we do not miss these professional duties.

The British Airways direct flight from Philadelphia to London leaves in fact around the scheduled time, after 6pm. At the check in, we see Paolo Fortina, world traveler, who is going to Turin just to see a rugby match on TV (!) with his friends, for the weekend. We later mock his love for British Airways, since the electronic TV and movie service does not work for the whole trip. It's probably a blessing, so that Paola, Andrea, Pietro, and I get to sleep for 2-3 hours each. We would have slept much longer, but the flight is 'only' 6 hours, about 2 hours less than going to Rome.

I also brush up on what I know about London and the U.K., so I can help mentor the kids and Paola when we visit historic sites. To review the history of England is to review a bit the history of the world. The Italians have had ancient Rome 2,000 years ago. The French peaked with Napoleon at the beginning of the 1800's. The English Queen Victoria reigned from 1837 all the way to 1901, when the English 'owned' or had major influence on much of the world.

At its height, the British Empire was the largest empire in history, with almost a quarter of the world's total land area, and with one-fifth of its population. As a result, its political, linguistic and cultural legacy is widespread. It was said that "the sun never sets on the British Empire", because its span across the globe ensured that the sun was always shining on at least one of its numerous territories.

October 21, Friday

Our flight is quick. We get woken up at 5am, which is just about midnight for us. The captain, lovely in his calm British accent, announces that we'll land at approximately 6am, as we are not allowed to do so before that time. So even if we took off about 30 minutes late, we land earlier than our 6:20am scheduled arrival time.

Our bags arrive very quickly and efficiently. I text Andrea Carrara, but I know that he won't be at work until at least 8am. Paolo Fortina is set to go and shower at the British Airways VIP lounge, and wait for his flight to Turin at 1pm. We, instead, are set to attack London, and make our way towards our apartment. Even if we cannot check in until 10am, we figure we'll have breakfast in central London, and not in the airport.

Paola is a wonderful travel companion. Not only she is extremely helpful with planning, hotels, etc. But she is also comfortable both in 5-star hotels as she is taking a public bus. In fact, our plan to move around in London is to use the subway, the famous London Tube. We ask for where to buy tickets, and, after some questioning regarding the various options, we buy 4 weekly tube passes, called Oyster cards. 37 pound each, including 5 pounds for 'top off'.

With 5 pieces of luggage, one each plus a larger one for me since I'm staying longer, we board the Piccadilly Line a few minutes after 7am. The ride from Heathrow will be over 1 hour and a half. One blip is the fact that the tube's driver at one station suddenly asks us to get off, given a fire in Arsenal Station. In the early 40-degree grey London morning, we have to figure out what other line to board. Part of the expected surprises of every trip; the good thing is, we are not in a rush. We eventually board the Bakerloo Tube line, and get off at Lambert Station, just south of the Thames.

I propose a taxi, but Paola wants to walk, despite the luggage we are logging along. It's just 9am, and the house is not available until about 10am, so we decide to stop at a café for breakfast. The Costa Café is just across the Lambert Station, and looks good, busy with Londoners queuing for hot chocolate and for croissants. I order one cappuccino for Paola, 3 hot chocolates for us boys, 2 long chocolate croissants for Paola and I, and other pastries for Andrea and Pietro.

Now London appears in the sun. Hard to imagine, but that what's in front of my eyes this glorious morning. As I look at my iPhone, which is working great, I see we are supposed to have sun for at least the next 5 days. In all of my prior trips to London I've seen mostly clouds and rain. London will be a different town to Paola, Andrea, and Pietro's eyes with this beautiful fall sunlight.

To get to our apartment, which is Flat D152, Parliament View, 1 Albert Embankment, London, SE1 7XQ, we walk about another 400 meters. We stroll along Thomas and Guy's Hospital, one of the most famous medical centers in the U.K., which I've heard much about. It's not easy to drag my larger suitcase on the uneven sidewalk and at times pebbled streets.

The apartment is called Riverview apartments because it's right on the river. We call the managers who are supposed to bring us the keys. They arrive in about 10 minutes, as we already begin to marvel at black taxis and red double decker buses, all driving on the left, and the magnificent views.

The apartment is well beyond our expectations. First, it is placed so near many of London's most famous sites. From our large living room window, we have a splendid view of the House of Parliament, with Victoria's Tower, and even Big Ben. The building looks fairly new, mostly glass and steel. The apartment is large, with 2 bedrooms; 2 bathrooms; a large kitchen with refrigerator, microwave, and dishwasher; laundry room; and magnificent living room with flat screen TV and dining table. We feel at home.

But London is waiting. One of the keys to 'beat' jet lag is to adjust right away to the new clock; to get outside in the sun, which is shining ever more brightly off the House of Parliament façade. I'm surprised that Paola does not even want to empty the suitcases and organize the apartment. After less than 20 minutes in the flat, and a few 'hooos' and 'haaaas' of happiness, we are off sightseeing.

We go and walk on the Southbank, and begin to take a few pictures of the House of Parliament, right there on the brink of falling in the north side of the Thames. I briefly begin to read some text from the Fodor guide I'll always carry with me, to erudite the kids, but also Paola and I. We cross from the Southbank to the Northbank at Westminster Bridge. Bobbies are manning the entrance to Parliament. Westminster Abbey is closed. Hordes of tourists are everywhere, often bumping into each other as they look up at the sites, most notably the Big Ben, instead of each other.

As the day is beautiful, and we are a bit tired already, we decide to go on a River Cruise. This would be a perfect, relaxing way to get an initial idea of the London geography and its major sites, many of which can be seen from the Thames. After having asked a female Bobby in front of the gate at the House of Parliament for information, we go back to the left, north side of Westminster Bridge, where boats take off for tours. I wish I had studied them a bit more. It's hard to decide from the many choices. We go for the one that seems most popular, without even checking the differences in prices (my papa' would have).

The river cruise lasts 3 hours, from about 12 noon to 3pm. We pass under all the main bridges, including London and Tower Bridge. London Bridge was bought by an American many years back, but he thought he was buying instead the more iconic Tower Bridge. Tower Bridge is only a little over 100 years old. Under Blackfriar's bridge, in 1982, Roberto Calvi dangled dead, the product of an international bank fraud involving, among many institutions, also the Vatican and Cosa Nostra.

The two guides on the River Cruise are actually pretty funny, with dry British humor. One describes how over 500 couples have been married in the London Eye. The ride lasts about 30 minutes. One can rent a cabin for about 1,000 pounds, which includes priest and ceremony. At the top of the ride, the 'I do's' are said, and the couple is pronounced husband and wife. Then the guide says, with perfect timing: "And it's all downhill from there."

There were several other occasions where the boat was brought to great laughter. Another I remember is when we went by the National Theatre. The building is an insignificant and unaesthetic accumulation of grey concrete. The guide stated: "It has been called the ugliest building in England. I disagree. [pause] I think it's the ugliest building in the world. In fact, even Prince Charles said this building is ugly. [pause] And Prince Charles knows what ugly is." More laughs.

Also, when we pass by a modern, oval-shaped, new building, covered in glass, the guide explains that this important site took millions of pounds to create. The city spent also 5 million pounds in tax money to come up with a unique name. After much thought, they settled on a brilliant name, "City Hall." More laughter.

We go by the Tower of London, one of the most visited tourist site of this huge city. This is where the 'modern' history of England began, in 1066. After Tower Bridge, we head for Greenwich, a 20 minute ride. The sun is highest above us, the guide stops talking, the ride is smooth. We all begin to feel drowsy. Some of us fall asleep.

Greenwich is a reminder of how powerful the British Empire was. The whole word sets their watches according to the mean solar time at the Royal Observatory of this little town. Maps of the world have usually England at its center, with the Americas on the left and Asia and Australia on the right.

Seeing London from the Thames teaches us how this town became so powerful and important, due to its river and geography. Look at a map of England. The bay where the Thames ends is well protected, and on the southeastern side of England there is less rain and precipitation than in most other parts of the British Isles.

The city of London was originally called Londinium, and founded about 43 AD by the Romans. Its initial, as well as later success was certainly due to its wonderful strategic position on the Thames, easily navigable.

As we come back from Greenwich, which is closer to the mouth of the river, we see an incessant bilateral succession of wharfs. In the prosperous years of the British Empire, goods coming from all over the known world, including the Americas, Asia and Africa, were docked safely in these wharfs. Each wharf specialized in a special product, such as sugar, spices, animals, luxury goods, precious metals, furniture, etc. My mind, dozing off and on, imagines how busy this river looked in the 1800's, with ships docked on each wharf, and furious trading going on.

While we are near the district of Whitechapel, the guide tells us briefly the popular story of Jack the Ripper. "Jack the Ripper" is the name of a serial killer active in these impoverished areas of London in 1888. His attacks typically involved female prostitutes. They became so famous because he would first cut their throats, and then remove abdominal internal organs. Mainly because of the extraordinarily brutal character of the murders, and because of media treatment of the events, the public came to believe in a single serial killer known as "Jack the Ripper".

While several investigations into this series of brutal killings were never able to connect all the killings to one assassin, the legend of Jack the Ripper solidified. As the murders were never solved, the legends surrounding them became a combination of genuine historical research, folklore, and pseudohistory. There are now over one hundred theories about the Ripper's identity, and the murders have inspired multiple works of fiction. Andrea and Pietro ask a few questions about this fascinating old story.

Another, more positive, story told by the guide is the fact that the Thames, while polluted and sick for centuries from the heavy traffic and dumping of toxic materials, is coming a bit back to life.

While empty of life a hundred years ago, currently 115 different types of fish, and several types of birds, live in the London Thames. We can see that certainly many birds right now are diving to its waters, convincing me that they are indeed finding some food in these light brown waters.

As we come off the boat cruise, we have two orders of business to attend to. First, have a bite to eat. Then, the kids want to head to Piccadilly Circus, where their good friend, Luca Fortina, has told them there is a large, famous sports store. On the dock, we find a public toilet, where, for 50 pence each, Andrea, Pietro, and I pee joyfully. Within 100 meters, we also find a small grocery store. We buy some yogurt, chips, small tuna sandwich, cookies, and we happily devour the light lunch while we continue heading for Piccadilly Circus.

We walk through White Hall, towards Trafalgar Square, which is on our way. Trafalgar Square is one of my favorite places in London. The square commemorates the Battle of Trafalgar, the biggest British naval victory ever. In 1805, Admiral Horatio Nelson defeated Napoleon at Cape Trafalgar, in the south-west of Spain, on the shore of the Atlantic Ocean, northwest of the Strait of Gibraltar. At the center of the square, towering over 200 feet high, there is Nelson's Column. Four lion statues at its base guard Lord Nelson.

The square is usually busy with people gathering around as well as passing by. It is used often for political demonstrations and community gatherings, such as the celebration of New Year's Eve. Now it's actually momentarily closed since an American Football theme park is being arranged in honor of the Chicago Bears – London Monarchs game to be played that weekend in London. I tell the kids about the history of Horatio Nelson and Napoleon, and how much I love these four huge dark lion statues at the corners of the large square.

Haymarket Street is lined with nice shops and some musical theaters, a small Broadway. Or, perhaps more correctly, the mother of the New York Broadway. I'm not sure. There is a nice, elegant, posh pastry store on the left side of Haymarket, with many beautiful cakes, but we resist from going in. Paola notices a small grocery store where we could come back to and buy some food for breakfast at the apartment. There is an imposing statue with horses at the corner of Haymarket and Piccadilly Circus, and the impression is that the horses could at any moment gallop over the crowd.

Piccadilly Circus is another one of my favorite spots in London, in the so called West End. It was named 'Piccadilly' apparently from 'piccadills,' or collars that a tailor with a shop here sold more than a couple of centuries ago. And 'Circus' because it is a circle, connecting several streets.

As we arrive to Piccadilly Circus, our attention is taken by the fountain, and by the Cool Britannia store, selling 'all things British.' We finally find Lillywhites Sports store. Suddenly, Andrea and Pietro have boundless energy. They gallop two floors up to the soccer floor. Full of soccer jerseys, socks, shorts, jackets, especially of Barclays Premier League teams, but also of many other famous international teams. The place is overtaken with thousands of teenager sport fans from all corners of the globe, including two from Philadelphia.

Andrea looks at all the cleats, but does not buy any, as Paola recently bought him a $80 pair, and he does not need two pairs. He is not too happy about this, even if he keeps his complaining passive. Pietro buys instead a white Inter jacket, and a Newcastle goalie shirt with his name and the number 1 stamped on the back. Excellent choices, which lighten my wallet by about 50 pounds. I had feared much more, after over one hour of roaming around by these two avid soccer fans.

While in the store, I get a call from Ignazio Marino. My great friend, senator and surgeon, is in town with his wife Rossana visiting their daughter Stefania. Stefania is a freshman at Queen Mary, at the University of London. They'd like to have dinner with us. I tell him our tentative plan was to have dinner with Olivier, and I feel silly being already overbooked in our first night in a foreign town.

Eventually I reach Olivier, who is thinking Japanese food for dinner with just him, his wife, Paola and I. We do not want to leave the kids alone, Japanese is not Paola's favorite, and I sense Olivier is set on this food. But it's easy to reschedule to Sunday brunch with them, so we'll see also his daughter Gabriella.

I call back Ignazio around 6pm, and schedule dinner at around 7pm. They would also like Japanese, but they are easily convincible to set for their second choice, fish and chips, exactly what we Berghella's had been hoping for. Now we just have to take the subway back to the apartment, freshen up quickly, and take the tube again.

From the apartment, we take again Bakerloo line north, to Oxford Circus, where we arrive with five minutes to spare! We are close to Bond Street. Mayfair is a nice neighborhood. We walk around for a few minutes looking at the elegant shop windows, with the boutiques luckily (for me) now closed. The text from Ignazio that they have also arrived comes quickly, and we run into them while in the pedestrian-only street.

Dinner is at a famous fish and chips restaurant. Company and food are superb. Stefania is doing well. Ignazio talks about his trips and humanitarian efforts in the Central Republic of the Congo. All 7 of us have fish and chips; the only difference is the type of fish. Most have cod, some halibut, as per the waiter's advice.

What a great day. When we get back by tube again to our roomy and elegant apartment, I quickly shower. We fall asleep like four babies, dreaming of the full day we have had, and the many more adventures ahead of us.

October 22, Saturday

Even if we are eager to see as much of London as possible, we democratically and unanimously decide not to set any alarm clock for Saturday morning. In fact, we wake up more or less together after 9am, having slept at least 10 hours, each of us. Of course, the last one to get up is Andrea, who is a sloth in the morning. We had bought croissants, chocolate milk, and many other goodies, which we now enjoy with the magnificent House of Parliament view.

We are free to go anywhere we want, as the day is up to us. We have still lots to see. The day looks gorgeous again, with bright sunshine. Is this London or Rome? Ignazio had suggested several times the night before to go together to the Tate Gallery. Paola and I agree this is a good option, as we can walk there and in the meanwhile see many other important sites. Plus, we'll have other days to head to the two top attractions, the Tower of London and Madame Toussauds, which Andrea and Pietro, respectively, had requested we visit during our stay.

While I wait for the rest of the team to get dressed, I study a bit better the story of the Tate Museum. This new museum, opened in 2000, hosts modern works collected by sugar magnate Sir Henry Tate. He opened the original museum, now called Tate Britain, in 1897, but this 'offspring,' the 'Tate Modern,' is even more fabulous than the original museum.

We walk along the Southbank, towards East. There are lots of people. In fact, it's a beautiful Saturday. We pass by the London Eye, otherwise known as the Millennium Wheel. The queue is long, and the time is limited, so we skip the ride. We get free Coca Cola Zero from a couple of young marketers. We walk by the National Theatre, which indeed is ugly even seen up close. Below it, a skate park and a blanket of graffiti on the cement walls, which make the building better-looking.

Along the Thames we encounter three Jamaican street performers. They have gathered up a decent crowd, so we decide to stay and check it out. All three of them are unbelievably talented, twisting in unimaginable ways. At the end of the show, one of them pulls both his legs over his head and sits in a pot. Another picks up the pot and brings him around, for the crowd to see. They are fun and smiley. We give them a couple of coins and continue on our way.

We arrive at the Tate Modern. Ignazio, Rossana, and Stefania arrive two minutes after us, perfect timing. We spend over two hours inside. We see in particular the 6th, and 5th floors. I'd like to take a guided tour, but I'm democratically overruled. The first experience with modern art is striking for Andrea and Pietro. The last museum they had visited was the Louvre, and this is quite a difference from the Monna Lisa or the Venus of Milo. Andrea is mesmerized by a picture with a beggar jerking off. Pietro loves a large mirror, meant to be a work of art. Paola likes the wave painting, which seems to move as you look at it.

We do try to get food at the 7th floor café, but it closes at 2:45pm, and we are just a bit late. So we step out of the Tate, tired and a bit hungry. We walk across the Millennium Bridge, a pedestrian only bridge. The Millennium Bridge is a stunning steel suspension bridge, linking Bankside with the City. I like it because there are no cars, and a human walking on it feels more respected by the world.

It is located between Southwark Bridge (downstream) and Blackfriar's Railway Bridge (upstream). The name comes from the fact that it was opened in 2000. While the southern end of the bridge is near the Globe Theatre, the Bankside Gallery and the Tate Modern, the north end is next to the City of London School and St Paul's Cathedral. The bridge alignment is such that a clear view of St Paul's south facade is presented from across the river, framed by the bridge supports.

We arrive at St Paul's Cathedral. Sitting on the outside benches, we attempt reading a bit about St Paul, but most of our efforts are in finding a place to eat. That's when 'Around me,' the iPhone app, comes most handy. Around the corner we find, and it's almost 3pm, the Cafe' Rouge, where we can have a relaxed late lunch. The best part is sitting down.

Pietro eats a big steak and fries. Andrea has the same. I have an onion soup, and a Nicoise Salad. Pietro also has a big chocolate cake, 'buonissima.' Paola also has an onion soup, and pate'. Ignazio only has a sliced tomato with onions, both raw. Stefania orders just a dessert. As Ignazio had paid for the fish and chips dinner the night before, I pay this round, happily. This was a good spot.

In front of St Paul's Cathedral, a few hundred demonstrators are chanting against capitalism and the rich. It's the famous '99%', manifesting against the '1%'. The Cathedral therefore is closed. We let Stefania take the tube back to campus. Then Paola's buys first a cake for Arturo, then some food for us at a deli. In the meantime, Andrea and I take a close look at the tents around St Paul, studying the behaviors of the protesters.

Then we split from the Marino family. We begin walking back towards the apartment, forgoing the tube to enjoy exploring this part of London that we have not seen yet.

We walk along Fleet Street first. I see one of the oldest pubs in London, in The City neighborhood, the Ye Olde Cheshire Cheese. After a square, Fleet Street becomes Strand Street, one of the most famous streets in London. By chance, we notice the original Old Twinings Store, where in 1706 this now large international tea company was started by Thomas Twining.

We also walk by King's College. Informally called King's, this is a famous public research university, and a constituent college of the federal University of London. King's has a claim to being the third-oldest university in England, having been founded by King George IV and the Duke of Wellington in 1829. In 1836 King's became one of the two founding colleges of the University of London.

The list of his illustrious graduates is impressive. Prime ministers and princes, presidents and politicians, from Jordan, France, England, Cyprus, Seychelles, Bahamas, Uganda, Iraq,

India, and just about every corner of the world. They graduated in theology, physics, science, law, engineering, and just about any topic of possible study. King's alumni in religion include the Nobel Peace Prize laureate and Archbishop Emeritus of Cape Town Desmond Tutu (Theology, 1966). Notable King's alumni in poetry and literature include the poet John Keats (Medicine), and Virginia Woolf (Philosophy).

King's alumni in the sciences include Nobel laureates Max Theiler and Sir Frederick Gowland Hopkins; polymath Sir Francis Galton; pathologist Thomas Hodgkin; pioneer of *in vitro* fertilization Patrick Steptoe; botanist David Bellamy; noted theoretical physicist Peter Higgs and the founder of the study of radioastronomy Professor EG Bowen. King's is also the alma mater of the founder of Bentley Motors, Walter Bentley. And the list goes on. I'm impressed.

We walk by Somerset House, a grandiose building which I know little about. It's on the south side of the Strand, overlooking the River Thames. The central block of the Neoclassical building, the outstanding project of the architect Sir William Chambers, dates from 1776–96. It has classical Victorian wings to north and south. The East Wing of Somerset House forms part of King's College London. It used to be a British Navy building.

Pietro sees the water fountains, and, as he did in Florida when he was about three years old, cannot help walking around them, this time without getting soaking wet. He is still a child, and I hope he'll always be like this, like I try to do.

On the Strand, we also walk by another legendary site, the Savoy Hotel. Built in 1889, it was the first luxury hotel in Britain, introducing electric lights, electric lifts, bathrooms inside the lavishly furnished rooms, constant hot and cold running water, and many other innovations. It established an unprecedented standard of quality in hotel service, entertainment and elegant dining, attracting royalty and other wealthy guests and diners. Winston Churchill, George Gershwin, Frank Sinatra, Edward VII, Enrico Caruso, Charlie Chaplin, Harry Truman, Judy Garland, Babe Ruth,

Laurence Olivier, Marilyn Monroe, John Wayne, Humphrey Bogart, Elizabeth Taylor, Barbra Streisand, The Beatles and numerous others have stayed here.

Eventually, we find what Andrea and Paola have been looking for: a store similar to Staples, called Ryman, where Andrea can buy some colored paper for a homework project.

Accomplished this task, tired, we take the tube back to the apartment. We are running a bit late, but we know Arturo is easy-going and won't mind. He is the one who first introduced Paola to me on October 29, 1993, in Philadelphia. He knew both me, from my prior time in Philadelphia during medical school, and Paola, who he had been enamored with for a while. He and other common friends had told both Paola and I, separately, that we were made for each other. I owe him my happiness.

We had to be at Arturo's at 7pm. We washed off quickly. We took first the brown Bakerloo line, and then the blue Piccadilly line north bound to the Bounds Green stop. We arrive at about 7:30. I immediately text Arturo we have arrived, and he picks us up five minutes later in front of the grocery store with his big friendly smile.

His house is nice. The best features are his wife Giorgia, and especially his three children, three boys, Matteo, 'Di' Pietro, and Simone. I feel at home. Arturo and I lived together for one year back in 1994-95, and I can still feel the depth of our relationship. A good friend is forever, even if geography separates one another.

Just like in the past, with his other girlfriends, Arturo is the cook, exclusively. He enjoys it, and is a master at it. Antipasto is served with lots of tasty sausages, and cheeses. Then pasta (penne) with smoked salmon, cucumber and something that looks like thin grass. Second course is lamb and potatoes; and then the chocolate cake we had brought.

Arturo and Giorgia's kids are loud, and they clearly want more attention. Only later on they quiet a bit when our Pietro joins the three younger boys and plays with them. We have so much to catch up with: old good common stories, updates on friends, how our professional and personal lives have been in the last few years. Good old times are great to reminisce. Andrea stays with us at the table, more mature and adult each day.

Of the common friends, perhaps none is closer to us than Biagio. We decide to give him a call, all the way to Los Angeles. His voice is moved by our call, and warms our hearts.

We could spend many more relaxed hours together. We visit the house, and Andrea even gets to print some homework from the computer. The garden is very nice.

We end up taking the last tube back available to our apartment, as the subway in London stops at 12:30am. We finally get to sleep at 1am.

October 23, Sunday

Once again, we take it easy in the morning. The plan is to have brunch with Olivier, around 12:30pm. Pietro and I, as usual, wake up first. We turn the TV on, as we are both fans of this entertainer. I remember the excitement of Paolo Fortina for the Rugby World Cup final, which should have started, in New Zealand, at about 9am Greenwich-Mean Time (GMT). In fact, when we turn the TV on, BBC is transmitting live the latter part on the second half of 2011 Rugby World Cup Final, from Auckland, New Zealand.

The All Blacks, New Zealand's mythical team, is playing against France, and winning. Richie McCaw is the All Blacks captain. His face is all cut up and bloody already, and represents the game of rugby, as I explain to Pietro, and later, when he wakes up, Andrea. In the meanwhile, we have a wonderful family breakfast in our cozy apartment, looking at the House of Parliament, again illuminated by the unusual fall sun.

Twenty-four years after their last World title, the All Blacks win: the final score is 8-7. I feel bad for Olivier, who I'm sure has watched. 'Pauvre' France. But it's like if Brazil had just won the Soccer World Cup: when the legendary team of a nation obsessed with the sport wins, it's never a regret for me. The stadium and the whole nation of New Zealand are broadcast on TV, in sheer elation.

We get to South Kensington station with just one tube change, from the Bakerloo Line (third stop to Embankment) to the 'Green Line' (fourth stop). Olivier lives in Chelsea. As we walk the 200 or so yards towards his house, we enter the magical architecture of this enchanted neighborhood.

The streets are lined with elegant three story houses, sparkling white, all kept up to the T, seeming just painted the day before. Each has two white columns in the front, behind an elegant small garden, with green grass, neatly trimmed, typical of London.

We walk, always following the GPS on my iPhone, to Oslow 2, Chelsea. I look up across the street as I realize the even numbers are there. And I see immediately Olivier's smiley face, waiting for us on the steps of his stylish palace, the most elegant house on the street.

Olivier is a great friend. We have known each other since 1984, when we met in college, at Manhattanville, in New York. He and his identical twin brother James are the sixth and seventh sons of 'mama'', as they call her, a sweet American girl from Kansas, and Monsieur de Givenchy. Their dad was (he died a few years ago, unfortunately) the only brother of Hubert de Givenchy, the internationally famous designer, who dressed the world, including the unique Audrey Hepburn. His castle in France is full of antiques, and looks like Versailles.

Olivier and James were born in Bouvier, France, and only came to the States in 1983, when his dad, remarried, moved to Greenwich, Connecticut, to manage the Givenchy empire in the U.S. After college, James worked in the Givenchy store on 75th and Madison, in Manhattan. It goes without saying that these two handsome, friendly, French-accent speaking boys, were the most sought-after items in a small college full of gorgeous and somewhat easily-available girls.

They claim that, when I arrived to Manhattanville during their junior year, things changed. I do not think so, or at least did not realize it. Olivier was going out with a lively, beautiful Panamanian, Patricia Dutari. As usual, with all his relationships, he was a gentleman with her, and treated her as every girl should be treated. He stayed in her apartment most of the time.

A brief episode summarizes his affairs. I saw him walking down the hallway in front of my room, bent on himself under a small fridge. 'Lolo, se qui se passe?' (Olivier, what's going on?), I asked. 'Patty and I just had a fight. I'm moving out temporarily, but (he smiled) I'll be back in there soon,' he answered in English, knowing my French is not that great.

Olivier eventually became a major banker, now for many years at JP Morgan. He manages tens of million of dollars for the rich, and often famous. First, he lived and worked in New York.

There he married Christine, and I was their best man at the civil ceremony, downtown at New York City Hall near where I did my residency. I was dressed in scrubs and white coat with a New York Downtown Hospital badge when pictures were taken. They had two gorgeous kids, Gabriella and Nicholas. Olivier has now been in London for over a decade. This is his town. And he has a new life.

Coming down the steps of Olivier's house at 2 Oslow, Chelsea, is beautiful Zoe, his new wife, Australian. I have been hearing about her for quite a while. I unfortunately missed their fabulous (as I could tell from the many pictures) Bahamas wedding. Zoe is good looking, tall, green eyes, assertive. After a big hug, and introductions, we visit the house, elegant as Zoe and Olivier both are. The house has also a perfect backyard for a two-on-two soccer game. But this would not be the right time, or the right way to impress Zoe.

We all walk a few yards through Chelsea, where everything is chic. The boys and girls coming out of church are all dressed impeccably, girls with perfect pastel colored dresses, boys with khaki pants, white shirts, light blue v-neck neat sweaters, fresh from Oxford or Bond Street boutiques.

James has told me Olivier will soon have a knee operation. I can tell he is limping a lot more than usual. When he was a little boy, Olivier's left leg was caught in a lawn mover. At least 10 inches of this leg, all around the knee, have major scars, of which Lolo has always been a bit self-conscious. He has already had two operations on it. Clearly this episode has marked not only his skin, but even more deeply his own soul. I wish him luck with his next surgery, necessary now because of his arthritis.

We stroll to lunch to a nice street market. To my delight, we can eat outside. Our table is soon joined by Gabriella, Olivier's daughter, now 17. The last time I had seen her was during their vacations in Connecticut, at a fancy country club. She is not a little girl anymore; she is a beautiful young dame. Her long blond hair, and especially her gracious deportment and movements, remind me of her maternal genes. I have her on my right, and Zoe in front. I must admit I have to make an effort to make sure I give enough attention to each, as both deserve my full interest.

Later, Massimo joins us at the table. He is one of Olivier's good friends in London. He is a bachelor (past two divorces), with a smile always on his face. He has been in the past the agent of models all over the world.

I loose myself a bit in Zoe's green eyes. I have few precious moments to get to know her. Uninhibited as is in my demeanor, I ask her about her story, her life. She is not shy in the answers. She has had a full life already, and is certainly mature, and very self-confident. When Paola and I invite them to come and visit, she replies 'Why would I ever come to Philadelphia', not mincing words. I'm glad, really glad, she wants kids, as I'm not afraid to ask her. Olivier is a good father, has the money, a big heart, and will have even more time for future kids. I love reproduction and its consequences.

Olivier and I recall the good old college days, and we mention Nabil, our good Lebanese college mate now in Ghana. Lolo tells everyone how I used to botch the name Piccadilly Circus when I came to Nabs' wedding, calling it 'Ciccacilly Pinkus', or 'Miccadilly Virtus', or something like that, obviously to make them all laugh. Food is good, with pizza as appetizer. Pietro and Andrea have non-alcoholic margheritas. I have a Nicoise salad, but I can never find it as good as the one I had in Malaysia years ago.

Gabriella is good-looking, beautiful and sophisticated like Christine, with Olivier's round face and I think his color eyes. She is tall, with a nice demeanor, and seems sweet like her dad. Zoe later says the book I wrote was wonderful. I can't figure out what she read; then she says 'From father to son.'

I'm honored, glad, and see another good, excellent side of Zoe, as her compliment I can tell is very sincere. But I realize I just gave them another copy of this book ... had I given James an extra 'From father to son' copy to give to his brother in the past?

Maybe one of the best things in life I've done is find a few very good friends. Lunch passes quickly. It's like Olivier and I have always lived in the same building, the same town, even if over 25 years have passed since the last time we did. As one is proud of his old attractive girlfriends, I'm even more proud of being friends with such outstanding boys, now men, as Olivier.

We leave each other's company, as they retire to their house. Olivier confides he'll take a nap. Life is full of compromises, and I'd made one with Andrea and Pietro. As avid soccer fans, and Premiership lovers, they wanted to see a game here during our UK stay. The compromise between them, me, and Paola, was that we would get to watch a bit of the most important game of that weekend.

So we walk back to a nice pub we had seen on our way to the market, with a large flat screen monitor pointed towards the sidewalk. We (Andrea, Pietro, me, and even Massimo, 'interista' like us) watch Manchester United – Manchester City. We arrive at half-time, the score is 0-1. We see the replay of the goal in the first half, a Balotelli beautiful 'piatto destro' to the far post. Massimo and I order two lagers, to blend with the Chelsea crowd.

The second half is incredible. In the first few minutes, Johnny Evans is given a straight red card for a last-man fault to Balotelli. The second MC goal is Balotelli's, again! A tap-in from a great cross from Milner after a great heel pass from Silva.

Then 0-3, Kun Aguero. Then 1-3 from an incredible shot from the 18 yard line to the right upright from Fletcher. The game is completely open now, both teams attacking, but MU with few defenders and in great difficulty with the fast and furious MC counter attacks. 1-4 from Dzeko, a great pass from Silva, again. 1-5 David Silva, under DeGeia's legs. 1-6 Dzeko: corner kick, Kolarov header, pass from Lescott from the line to hit Dzeko's knee, and in. I could not have dreamed a more exiting game to watch in the sun, in a London pub with my two adored boys.

Paola had waited for us patiently in a near-by park, reading the Fodor's guide. I had been texting Raffaella, as we had tentatively arranged to try to meet that afternoon. We plan to meet in Hyde Park. Pietro is a bit fed up with the tube, so we oblige to his request to finally board one of the elegant and typical black London taxis. The fact that we can sit two across from the other two, in front of each other, with plenty of space, makes the ride special and classic.

We arrive in front of Royal Albert Hall, as per Raffa's instructions. We wait a bit on the steps of Albert Memorial, watching Londoners stroll by in this south street of Hyde Park. Albert was the beloved husband of Queen Victoria. As for most historic positive figures, her success is certainly in part due to happiness in her personal life. Raffa, her husband Charles, and their sons James and Alex, with dog included, arrive.

We all walk together in Hyde Park. It's almost 4 o'clock, a beautiful fall afternoon in the park. We decide to head towards Kensington Palace. While Raffaella walks mostly with Paola, I catch up with Charles, a quintessential English gentleman. I've always liked him. He has a calm and unassuming demeanor, which I admire. While married well (Raffaella is attractive, and her dad was mayor in Pescara and also an Italian Senator), he is not pretentious, but rather humble.

Raffa, Paola, me, and the kids go and visit Kensington Palace. King William III acquired it in 1689 from his Secretary of State, the Earl of Nottingham. The King wanted a residence near London, but away from the smoky air of the capital, because he was asthmatic. This Royal residence has since then been populated with the British monarch family members. Perhaps the most famous resident here was Princess Diana, from 1981 to her death in 2002.

I hear the guide talk about the many stories of the Castle. The one that captures me the most is about Victoria. On June 20, 1837, as she wrote later in her diary, "I was awaken at 6 o'clock by Mamma, who told me the Archbishop of Canterbury and Lord Conyngham were here and wished to see me. I got out of bed and went into my sitting-room (only in my dressing gown), and, *alone*, saw them. Lord Conyngham then acquainted me that my poor

Uncle, the King, was no more, and had expired at 12 minutes past 2 this morning, and consequently that *I* am *Queen*."

She had shut the door in front of her mother, who had been an ally to the unfriendly Regent. She was only 18. She later married Albert, her sweetheart. She ruled for more than 63 years over a fourth of the Earth and a fifth of its inhabitants at the time, the largest empire ever. I love history.

After the Kensington Palace visit, brief as it was closing at 6pm, we depart from Raffa and her family, heading home since it is getting chillier and the boys, or more like it the mother, are getting cold. Olivier sends me a text message asking where we are. He has awakened from his nap. He comes to the Round Pond with Lilli, his dog, and with a big smile. So we spend a few more precious moments together. In a convertible mini cooper, he then takes off again, as we are getting ready to head off ourselves.

Raffaella has invited us for tea in Pimlico, at their house. So we walk to the tube station, but it is closed. We try to catch a cab, but it takes us at least 15minutes. We finally get one, and so arrive at 134 Cambridge Street, again in a beautiful neighborhood, lined with nice houses, all well kept.

Raffaella and Charles' house is large, elegant, very 'England'. We (the boys) all pee a storm. Our hosts offer us apple pie, tea with milk, cookies, Brunette jam with bread, which we devour, hungry. The four kids watch briefly some TV upstairs. Once again, the company of Charles and Raffaella is quite enjoyable. Raffa talks about all the people she interviewed through me for the medical magazine she collaborates with. Andrea gets to print more of his homework. Pietro also plays a quick game of chess, but has his queen (in England!) taken by James, the young son of Charles and Raffa. As we depart, after 7pm, Raffaella even gives us some kish to take with us for dinner.

We are not that far from our apartment, so we walk. We get some pizza on the way, beer for Paola, and she even finds some fruit at the deli. We walk by Vauxhall, where two guys are kissing. This is clearly a gay neighborhood.

We have dinner in the apartment as a family – it is wonderful. Then Andrea does his homework, and Pietro and I write the skeleton of our trip so far, making sure we cover at least the main events. Another full, magnificent day.

October 24, Monday

Today we can finally dedicate ourselves fulltime to site-seeing. Andrea and Pietro both are hungry for tourism. Andrea is particularly fond of seeing the Tower of London, and Pietro Madame Tussauds. So those are our priorities. It's again a beautiful day. We have not seen a drop of rain in four straight days in London!

We walk this time along the Southbank of the Thames to Westminster Bridge, and then down to Westminster Station. The yellow and green tube lines go directly to Tower Hill. As one gets out of the tube, the Towers and walls that make out the complex of the Tower of London, appear just after going under a bridge. One turns right to a slight uphill, with the complex on the left.

We buy tickets, and get to the entrance. Then we wait for the 10:30am tour guide, a Beefeater. I had heard there is nothing better than a Beefeater to tell the kids about this enchanted castle. Andrea in the meanwhile reads from the Fodor's guide. He reads with a British accent, which Pietro has a mastery of, and Andrea is quickly leaning to imitate as well.

Andrea reads the story of the Beefeaters, now 35 Yeoman Wardens, in place since the 14th century. They were at some point in history possibly paid in beef, which the common people in London could not afford. The term 'beefeater' was therefore derogatory, and stated the anger of the people at the privileges of these guards.

Of course our Beefeater says they are paid 'peanuts' now, so the name should be changed to 'Peanuteaters'! As he says his jokes, he makes all kinds of faces, like a little kid, even if he must be at least 60 years old and is about 6 foot 1 inch, taller than me with the Beefeater hat.

The Beefeater has a strong voice. Later he coughs a couple of times, it's hard trying to be heard by over 100 people in open spaces with lots of extra noise from other tourists. The choice of a

Beefeater guide is great. He is a wealth of information. At the Middle Tower, the main entrance and our first stop, he tells us about the founding of the Castle.

William the Conqueror had defeated Edward the Confessor at the battle of Hastings in 1066. He feared the revenge of the Londoners, so he first sent only a few Normans to begin to build a castle in the best place, along the river Thames, so to control the town. He eventually was invited by some London aristocrats to enter the City. The White Tower, a huge building started probably around 1068-1070, was finished around 1100. Over time this first Norman kings built the inner walls of what is now known as the Tower of London, then the outer walls, and the many towers around.

The tower of London has been the king's residence, a castle for defense, a prison (as early as 1100), a place for torture, an armory for warlike provisions, the treasury for the crown jewels, a Coin Mill, etc. Isaac Newton in fact was the headmaster at the coin mill. It's interesting that Albert Einstein was a patent clerk when in 1905 he had is 'Annus mirabilis.' You can have a boring job and have time for your real passion, for both of them physics. You do not need special help or time to change the world.

The beefeater makes us imagine the times in the late 1000's, when William the Conqueror and his court established themselves at the Tower. They were speaking French, he tells us, with a funny face of disgust. You can tell he considers it a minor language compared to his royal English.

The second stop is at the corner below the Bell Tower, where the Beefeater again climbs to higher ground (a pillar about a foot high) and starts telling us more stories. The road on our left is where the residences for the Beefeaters are. He looks at the many kids in our large group, most just in front of him, and tells them, with great actor's suspense, that that the sign on front of his door reads: "Beware you who enter."

He goes on describing the different buildings making up the large complex, and then states: "Americans, think, if you paid your taxes this would still all be yours..." With his usually funny British-humor face.

Then his (and our) third stop is at the Traitors' Gate. Originally this was the entrance for Kings, directly from the river Thames, easy and protected. This later became way in for many who were brought here to be imprisoned and executed. It was the entrance for the three queens killed here: Anne Boleyn, Catherine Howard, and Lady Jane Grey.

Anne Boleyn first walked in this gate to Tower of London as a queen. She was Queen of England from 1533 to 1536 as the second wife of Henry VIII of England. Her story is quite remarkable. She was a commoner, who became maid of honor to Henry VIII's first wife and queen, Catherine of Aragon.

Henry VIII soon began courtly pursuit of Anne. She resisted his attempts to seduce her, refusing to become his mistress as her sister Mary had. It soon became the one absorbing object of Henry's desires to annul his marriage to Queen Catherine so he would be free to marry Anne. When it became clear that Pope Clement VII would not annul the marriage, the breaking of the power of the Catholic Church in England began.

Henry and Anne married in 1533. As a result of this marriage and the excommunications that followed, the first break between the Church of England and Rome took place. The Church of England was brought under the King's control. Anne soon gave birth to the future Elizabeth I of England. To Henry's displeasure, however, she failed to produce a male heir. Henry was not totally discouraged, for he said that he loved Elizabeth and that a son would surely arrive. Three miscarriages followed, however, and by March 1536, Henry was courting Jane Seymour.

Henry had Anne investigated for high treason in 1536. On May 2nd, she was arrested and sent to the Tower of London. So, as the Beefeater says, she was brought back three years later through the same gate, but this time to be ultimately decapitated. She was tried before a jury of peers and found guilty. She was beheaded four days later on Tower Green. Modern historians view the charges against her, which included adultery and incest, as unconvincing.

Following the coronation of her daughter, Elizabeth, as queen, Anne was venerated as a martyr and heroine of the English Reformation. Anne has been called the most influential and important queen consort England has ever had, since she provided the occasion for Henry VIII to divorce Catherine of Aragon, and declare the independence of the Church of England from Rome.

Catherine Howard was the pretty fifth wife of King Henry VIII and the cousin of Anne Boleyn. Henry called her his 'Rose without a Thorn', and showered her with gifts and public affection. After her wedding to Henry VIII, who was an old, repulsive, obese man, she had an affair with the young and handsome Thomas Culpepper. And was found out. King Henry was devastated. Catherine was arrested at Hampton Court for adultery. Her lovers were executed and she passed their gruesome, impaled heads on London Bridge on her way to Traitor's Gate, the entry to the Tower of London. She was just 18 years old when she was herself beheaded there in 1542.

Lady Jane Grey is also known as The Nine Days' Queen, as she reigned only from July 10th to 19th, 1553. When King Edward VI laid dying in June 1553, he nominated Jane as successor to the Crown in his will, thus subverting the claims of his half-sisters Mary and Elizabeth under the Third Succession Act. During her short reign, Jane resided in the Tower of London. She became a prisoner there when the Privy Council decided to change sides and proclaim Mary as Queen on 19 July 1553. Lady Jane Grey was executed, only 16 or 17 years old. All three queens were reserved the privilege to loose their heads not in public at Tower Hill, but inside the walls of the Tower of London, in Tower Green.

At the fourth stop, the Beefeater tells us the most famous story of the Bloody Tower, pointing to it. Perhaps this is the most famous story of this Tower, and one of the most infamous stories in all of British monarchal history. It makes one understand the brutal means to assure oneself the succession to the title of King of England.

The Princes in the Tower is a term which refers to Edward V of England and his younger brother Richard. The two children were the only sons of Edward IV of England alive at the time of their father's death in 1483. In May 1483 Edward, then 12 years old, and Richard, 9, arrived in London for Edward's coronation, and were accommodated in the Tower of London, then a royal residence.

But their own uncle Richard Duke of Gloucester had a different plan. Both princes were declared illegitimate by an Act of Parliament in 1483, known as *Titulus Regius*. Their uncle Richard was crowned as Richard III. There are no reports of the two princes being seen after the summer of 1483. Their fate remains an enduring mystery, but historians and contemporary popular opinion agree that the princes were probably murdered in the Tower. There is no record of a funeral.

In 1674, the skeletons of two children were discovered under the staircase leading to the chapel, during the course of renovations to the White Tower. On the orders of Charles II the remains were reburied in Westminster Abbey. In 1933, the grave was opened to see if modern science could cast any light on the issues. The skeletons were determined to be those of two young children, one aged around seven to eleven and the other around eleven to thirteen.

Then our Beefeater makes us stop almost at the top of the stairs towards the plaza around the White Tower. The White Tower is a central stone tower, the old keep, at the Tower of London. It dominates these surroundings. Its construction began around 1078.

Then we stop a few steps further, still near the White Tower, at a small square. This is adjacent the Tower Green, the location where the seven 'lucky' victims not to be killed on Tower Hill, including Anne Boleyn, were decapitated. In this location, now there is a modern glass and steel piece, clearly not liked by the Beefeater.

Then we go into the Chapel Royal of St Peter ad Vicula. We are the only one allowed in, following our expert guide. Andrea, Pietro, Paola, and I seat in front in the first bench. The Beefeater, not more than three yards in front of us, tells us all the story of the Chapel, originally catholic. The three queens killed here in the Tower complex are buried around the altar. The Beefeater ends his wonderful instructional conversation telling us that, for him, our 'group has been the group most... most... most recent!' Again, with a funny smirk. I'm a bit sad we are done with the Beefeater, even if this last joke was perhaps the worst one.

We then walk in the White Tower. The building itself is interesting. Almost as if to still prove its inexpugnability, visitors can access it only from an outside staircase which leads directly to the second floor. Inside, the main attraction is the Armoury Museum. We are a bit tired, but I see Andrea and Pietro busy looking at all different kinds of armor. There are big ones, small ones for kids, leg pieces, arm pieces, breast pieces, hand pieces, foot pieces, swords, armor for horses. They are made of different metals, often of heavy iron. Helmets are finished in many different shapes, and one wonders often how the soldier could see anything from the small slit for vision.

The Crown Jewels are housed in the Waterloo Barracks. Andrea and Pietro are very impressed at their sight. There is a moving floor on both sides of the elevated display windows, where tourist can stand and spend a few seconds in front of each piece. It is remarkable to be able to be so close to them, especially thinking that these inestimable jewels were almost stolen in 1671. The most breathtaking display is that of the crowns themselves.

Elisabeth II was crowned with St Edward's Crown. This crown, made in 1661, is very heavy, and only used for coronations, so it has been jobless since 1953. The lighter Imperial State Crown is used every year by the Queen at the State Opening of Parliament. It was made in 1937, for George VI, and includes the legendary

'Stuart Sapphire', the 'Black Prince Ruby', and 'Queen Elisabeth's Pearls'. These gems are all too big for me to believe that they are real, but indeed they are. This crown alone contains 2,868 diamonds, 17 sapphires, 11 emeralds, 5 rubies, and 273 pearls.

In the Sovereign's Sceptre with Cross, is set Cullinan I, also called the First Star of Africa. This is the largest top quality diamond in the world, weighting over 530 carats. In the Crown of The Queen Mother, made in 1937 for the wife of George VI, is set the famous Koh-i-noor.

At the end, Paola and I state we have seen everything we needed to see. Perhaps the only thing we have missed is seeing some instruments of torture. Walking down the stairs towards the exit, at the Bloody Tower, we see a sign for 'Torture'. We cannot resist from walking in. There a medium size room, inside the Wakefield Tower, with three main instruments of torture shown. Not much compared to what Paola and I saw in Tuscany in San Gimignano.

The first instrument of torture is called the Scavenger's Daughter. It consist of an iron frame formed of a base-plate and two semi-circular bows. The bows were fastened tightly across the prisoner's back, holding him or her in a crouched position, with his/her arm against his/her sides. One would have to bend on himself, and then this small metal cage would be constricted around the victim.

The second torture instrument is perhaps the scariest. In fact, the Rack was the Tower of London's most infamous instrument of torture. It consist of a large iron frame containing three wooden rollers. One warder could operate it by turning the central roller with a lever. Ropes ran to the other rollers at the head and foot of the rack, making them turn in opposite directions. The central roller also had an iron ratchet and teeth, holding it in position and keeping the victim stretched. So the Rack pulls one's arms superiorly, the legs inferiorly, breaking slowly all the joints without killing the victim. Who things of these things?

The last instrument consists of menacles. These are iron rings, bolted high to the wall by metal chains attached to a piece of wood, and fastened around the victim's wrists. From the menacles, the prisoners could be left hanging above the ground. Apparently the victim again would not die, but, at best, would then not be able to use his hands for days. Sigh.

We walk out, and I'm hungry, and ready for food and rest. As Paola and Andrea do not want to eat yet, Pietro and I get a quick twister (soft ice cream) for two pounds each. When I have it in my hand, I notice that it is small, not very good, a tourist trap. Paola declines fish and chips (indeed another tourist trap, and expensive). We fetch the tube again, direct to Baker Street station on the Circle Line (yellow), and get a bit if sitting down in the ride.

Paola does not believe we are taking the right train, but a kind Indian Englishman with family has told me the Circle line towards Liverpool station is indeed what we need to take, the one right on our platform.

As we step out of the station, Pietro is the one who first spots the entrance to Madame Tussauds. Well, he is the one who had this visit as first on his list of our 'things to see in London.' We cross the street. We look right, look left: why do the British drive on the wrong side of the street?

This is a fascinating story. For an Italian and American like me, born on the 1960's, right-hand traffic has been the norm. One would assume it was always so. But, this is far from the truth. The rule in ancient Greece, Egypt and Rome was the keep-left rule. This is proven by several facts. For examples, in front of shops, ancient Romans drove on the left, since carts would exit the quarry heavily loaded, and enter it empty, leaving very different marks.

Ancient travelers on horseback generally rode on the left side of the road. As more people are right-handed, a horseman would be able to hold the reins with his left hand and keep his right hand free, so to offer in friendship to passing riders or to defend himself with a sword, if necessary.

In the late 18th century, the shift from left to right that took place in countries such as the United States was based on teamsters' use of large freight wagons pulled by several pairs of horses. The wagons had no driver's seat, so a postilion sat on the left rear horse and held his whip in his right hand. Seated on the left, the driver preferred that other wagons pass him on the left so that he could be sure to keep clear of the wheels of oncoming wagons. He did that by driving on the right side of the road

Over the course of the 20th century, there was a gradual worldwide shift from driving on the left to the right, mostly from the late 1920's to the 1940's. So, though originally most traffic drove on the left worldwide, today about 66% of the world's people live in right-hand traffic countries and 34% in left-hand traffic countries. About 72% of the world's total road distance carries traffic on the right, and 28% on the left.

To my begging, we stop first at a small bar/restaurant to get a bite to eat. It's not a great stop in terms of the food quality, but we are sitting outside in a pleasant sunny early afternoon a few yards from the museum. My tuna sandwich is ok, and I also get some tapas which are eatable. But Pietro only takes a bite of his hotdog saying the ketchup is bad tasting. Andrea only eats about one fifth of his pastry, saying there is jam inside and it does not taste good. Paola finishes her sandwich, Pietro his 'replacement' lunch, a different sandwich. Andrea eats little, but in these teenage times he is so focused on being thin and good-looking that Paola and I cannot force him to eat any more than what he accepts to.

At Madame Tussauds we beat the line, since I've been smart enough to buy tickets at a shop at the exit of the Tower of London, for a small discount in pounds, but a major one in time. We stay in 'queue' for less than 10 minutes before entering the most expensive of London's attractions.

The first wax statues one encounters after the entrance are Hollywood stars. John Travolta is really life-like, even if one stands right next to it. Andrea is impressed that in front of a woman (made out of wax) who is taking a picture by aiming her camera towards the wax statue of Cristina Aguilera, many people duck, not wanting to obstruct the picture!

We see also Susan Sarandon, Nicole Kidman, Sean Connery, David and Victoria (ex-Spice) Beckham. Paola says she is taller than in life, but her long dress covers her shoes, I suspect with very high heels. Close to them we see Tom Cruise, then George Clooney. Angelina Jolie and Brad Pitt do not look to me like the real ones (like if I know). Pietro takes a picture with Jennifer Lopez. Paola does not want to sit next to George Clooney.

Next are Marlon Brando (one can barely tell it's him), Arnold Schwarzenegger (big guy), the great Robin Williams (Andrea takes a picture next to him), Shrek, Drew Barrymore, and Marilyn Monroe. I prefer to take a picture sitting next to a regal and sophisticated Audrey Hepburn, holding hands with her. James Dean does not look like in movies or pictures, while Humphrey Bogart dressed in white is impressive.

The next large room has the theme of sports. Tiger Woods is at the entrance of this section, all by himself. We easily recognize Cristiano Ronaldo, the Portuguese soccer star from Real Madrid. Then Pele': Andrea and Pietro take a great picture around him, hugging him. There is Jesse Owens representing the sprinters, while Boris Becker is only tennis player. I wonder why, then think that he won Wimbledon when only 17, and must have remained in British minds more than other champions with more trophies. Jose' Murinho, the famed soccer coach, is standing tough by a column, and I take another great picture with Andrea and Pietro next to him. We shoot some soccer balls towards moving targets, with no success.

Next are the scientists. The first one is Isaac Newton, present everywhere in London. Albert Einstein is a small smiling guy. Close to him there is a seated Picasso. So soon we have moved to artists, as I recognize near the wall one of my favorites, Vincent Van Gogh.

A huge space is reserved for singers. First, of course, the Beatles. Pietro takes a picture behind the couch where they are sitting looking jolly. Pietro also takes a picture strangling Justin Bieber. Then there are Michael Jackson, Rihanna, Lady Gaga, but no Madonna that I can see.

The world leaders are much more interesting to me. The first ones I admire, right next to each other, are Desmond Tutu, Gandhi, and Pope John Paul II. My impression is these were all nice men. Why do I take a picture next to Gandhi, and did not take one earlier next to Einstein? I admire and talk about Einstein all the time, but admire probably compassion as much a science. I appreciate caring for the poor and needy as much as scientific quest – be this way.

Later there are some British leaders, such as Tony Blair, Winston Churchill, Margaret Thatcher, David Cameron (prime minister now), and the apparently popular current major of London, Boris Johnson.

Next are leaders of the world, first current and then historic, such as Nicolas Sarkozy, Angela Merkel, and Barack Obama (prominent large statue behind the Oval Office desk, but it does not look like him). Then John Fitzgerald Kennedy, George W. Bush, close to him Adolf Hitler, later even Nelson Mandela. In this last group, I do not get how they were placed somewhat close to each other.

The tour at Madame Tussauds has been lots of fun. But we are tired. After exiting, fighting to get across thousands of tourists in the street, we get to the tube station, just around the corner. In our lovely apartment, we enjoy a brief period of relax.

Our discussion then turns on where to go to eat. We actually have lots of ideas, options, and suggestions from friends and from tour guides. As we are indeed tired, we decide to go to a restaurant close by that we can walk to. Our choice falls on Il Quirinale. A fancy Italian restaurant right next to the House of Parliament. I know it won't be cheap, but the kids had a terrible lunch, and deserve a great dinner.

As we are walking across the Lambert Bridge, Paola states we should call Andrea Carrara, who we know is around tonight, to see if perhaps he wants to come to dinner with us. I call him. To my delight, he agrees to join us. He sounds so exited, what a super-nice guy. I hope Pietro and Andrea will be a bit like him as they grow up.

We get to the restaurant a few minutes before the time of our reservation. As we walk along Great Peter Street, Paola and I notice a house for sale. It's three stories tall, has a small garden in front, and looks really elegant. As we pick the information pamphlet, we realize it's a mansion, selling for over 2 million pounds. Dreaming is great.

We all have a lovely dinner at Il Quirinale. Andrea Carrara arrives quickly, impeccably dressed with his signature v-neck blue sweater, so simply stylish, as he is. The food is wonderful, first rate authentic Italian dishes. We all have great pastas and second courses of fish and meat. The waitresses are Italian, speak perfectly our language, and behave in the typical kind British way. The restaurant is quiet, elegant, and our conversation is lively, happy.

We see the first and only rain during our trip going back from Il Quirinale to our 'royal' apartments in the Riverside across Lambert Bridge. Andrea Carrara runs off to his car. Another wonderful day.

October 25, Tuesday

This is the last day in London for Pietro, Andrea, and Paola. The night before Paola and I have already quickly started to prepare our luggage, as I'm going off to Liverpool in the afternoon, when they'll instead head towards Heathrow and their transatlantic trip back to Philadelphia.

We have planned to get up at 9:00am, and at least visit Westminster Abbey. After the last shower and breakfast at our royal Riverside apartment, we walk on Southbank towards Westminster Bridge, and I'm thinking just how familiar these sites have become for us in just a few days.

We get to Westminster Abbey just before 10:30am, and are extremely relieved to find almost no queue at all, may be ten people in front of us only. Once I get closer to the check-in counter, I notice that they have a list of times when guides are available. I see the first one is at 10:30am. That's in one minute! I inquire the clerk to which I pay the entrance fee. She seems nice, and tells me to wait a second. She checks with a person dressed win a black robe, and he says that's ok. We pay just three pounds more each to follow the guide.

Everything in this trip goes too well. By seconds, we are then allowed to go with the excellent guide who starts at 10:30am, only about eleven tourists total (he could have taken up to 20). I wonder why other people have not signed up!! They are crazy!!

The private guided tour takes one and a half hour. The tour guide, as I said, is dressed in a black robe, but tells us right away he's not clergy. He is the senior vicar for Westminster, and he is the longest serving vicar and guide at Westminster. He seems to know absolutely everything about the place.

The name Westminster may come from 'minister in the west,' meaning the clergy in the western part of the old city of London. Westminster was originally built by Edward the Confessor between 1042 and 1052 as a royal burial church, the first Norman Romanesque church in England, and was consecrated on 28 December 1065. This Anglo-Saxon king of England was catholic, and in fact the church was originally dedicated to St Peter (and called St Peter's Abbey).

Only a week after the consecration, the Confessor died on 5 January 1066, and the next day he was buried in the church. He was proclaimed a Saint by the Vatican in 1161. Westminster Abbey soon became the site of burial of these Norman kings. The original church was demolished in 1245 to make way for King Henry III's new building, which still stands. He was the first king to be also buried in the Abbey. Around 1559, Westminster became Anglican (aka Episcopalian).

In Westminster, there are more than 3,000 tombs. Like many old churches, this is a big cemetery, with a lot of buried people. Among them, most of the Royals up to 1750 or so. Our guide shows us some of the most famous tombs. We see that of Charles Darwin, placed in a prominent place on the floor. The guide tells us that obviously Darwin has never been well liked by religious people. So it may seem surprising he is buried in Westminster, and in a place where most people would notice the marble slate with his name and dates of birth and death on the floor.

By the vicar explains to us that the priests probably did it on purpose, placing Charles Darwin, the father of evolutionism and therefore against religious creativism, in this major hallway so that every visitor could 'walk on him.' Darwin's tomb is incessantly being trampled on.

Isaac Newton's grave is right next to Darwin's, but much different. Newton is by far the most revealed scientist in all of U.K.'s history. His tomb is a mausoleum of sorts, not at all on the floor, but on a prominent wall, with the sarcophagus high up from the pavement. It's just beautiful, with a marvelous marble sculpture on top.

The monument is of white and grey marble. Its base supports a sarcophagus with large scroll feet and a relief panel. The latter depicts boys using instruments related to Newton's mathematical and optical work (including the telescope and prism), and his activity as Master of the Mint at the Tower of London.

Above the sarcophagus is a reclining figure of Newton, in classical costume, his right elbow resting on several books representing his great works. They are labeled 'Divinity', 'Chronology', 'Opticks' [1704] and 'Philo. Prin. Math' [Philosophia Naturalis Principia Mathematica, 1686-7)]. With his left hand he points to a scroll with a mathematical design (the 'converging series'), held by two standing winged boys. The background is a pyramid on which stands a celestial globe with the signs of the Zodiac, of the constellations, and with the path of the comet of 1680. On top of the globe sits a figure of Astronomy leaning upon a book.

The Latin inscription testifies how Isaac Newton is remembered: 'Here is buried Isaac Newton, Knight, who by a strength of mind almost divine, and mathematical principles peculiarly his own, explored the course and figures of the planets, the paths of comets, the tides of the sea, the dissimilarities in rays of light, and, what no other scholar has previously imagined, the properties of the colors thus produced. Diligent, sagacious and faithful, in his expositions of nature, antiquity and the holy Scriptures, he vindicated by his philosophy the majesty of God mighty and good, and expressed the simplicity of the Gospel in his manners. Mortals rejoice that there has existed such and so great an ornament of the human race! He was born on 25th December, 1642, and died on 20th March 1727.' Not a bad epitaph at all!

We also see the tombs of famous writers, most importantly William Shakespeare, and most recently an actor, Sir Lawrence Oliver, buried here as recently as 1989. In a long narrow room, at the northeaster far end of Westminster Abbey, are the tombs of several royals. The ones I'm most impressed by, and that I remembered from previous visits, are those of two half-sisters, Queen Mary and Queen Elisabeth I.

Queen Mary, who reigned from 1553 to 1558, was the only daughter of Catherine d'Aragon, first wife of Henry VIII. Mary was catholic, as her mother. She devoted her time on the throne to restore England to what she saw as the true religion, that centered in Rome. She became known as Bloody Mary, as she was responsible for about 300 Protestant victims. She never conceived an heir.

Queen Elisabeth I, who reigned from 1558 until 1603, was the only daughter of Anne Boleyn, second wife of Henry VIII. Elisabeth was protestant, like her mother and father. She proclaimed the patriotic necessity of Protestantism with unfailing vigor. Her long reign included also the works of Shakespeare, and the defeat of the great Spanish Armada in 1588, making the British Empire the only superpower of those times. Elisabeth refused to marry and did not have direct heirs. She knew that after her the son of Mary Queen of Scots, who she had executed in 1587, would reign. What a mess.

It's interesting that the two half-sisters Queens Mary and Elisabeth I of England are buried so close to each other, even if they were so different in so many ways. Then we see the tomb of James I, the monarch after Elisabeth I. As he was the son of Mary Queen of Scots, he was originally called James VI of Scotland, and then became in 1603 James I as the first king of both England and Scotland. This dynastic succession put an end to centuries of conflict between Scotland and England.

Our vicar tells us the interesting story of Oliver Crowell, buried in Westminster only for three years. He represents the only gap – from 1653 to 1658 - of republic in a long line before and after him of monarchy. As the Royal Crown was reinstated, he was taken out of his tomb, subsequently mutilated, decapitated, and thrown in the river by order of next king, Charles II. Westminster is still very much a royal stronghold.

Interestingly, there is a huge Oliver Cromwell statue on the north side of the House of Parliament, the site of democracy for the United Kingdom, and the tribute to this hero (for some) is only about 100 yards from the walls of Westminster. Cromwell is certainly one of the more controversial figures in all of British history, but recently voted one of the 10 most influential Britons ever.

The House of Parliament also has a beautiful equestrian statue of Richard I. He was called 'Coeur de Lion,' or Richard the Lionheart, even before his accession, because of his reputation as a great military leader and warrior. I grew up with the myth that being brave as 'Riccardo Cuor di Leone' was the most courageous anyone could be. He reigned from 1189 to 1199.

Our guide takes us to visit the earliest royal tombs in Westminster, which include that of Edward the Confessor, placed in the middle of the central Chapel which is named after him. He reigned from 1042 until 1066, when William the Conqueror then took over for the Normans. The Confessor was responsible for the building of Westminster.

Another tomb in the Chapel of Edward the Confessor is that of Edward I, which reigned from 1272 to 1307, and is remembered as the Hammer of the Scots. Andrea and I kneel down and pray in one of the small niches inside the Confessor's tomb. This is one of the oldest parts of Westminster.

Our wonderful lead tells us myriads of other interesting stories. Among them, he explains the origin of the name 'Bobbies' for the British police. It was in fact Sir Robert Peel who, while Home Secretary, founded the metropolitan police in 1829. From his name, Robert, policemen in England are often referred as to 'Bobbies.' The vicar of course tells us this story as we admire Sir Robert Peel's tomb.

The guide is clearly in love with the monarchy, which infuses the atmosphere at Westminster. He is an Indian adopted by an English couple, and has been working for 16 years at Westminster Abbey. He is currently the most senior of these vicars. He has the outmost respect for anything to do with the royal family, and royal stories.

He asks us if we saw the royal wedding of Kate Middleton and Prince William. For that occasion, 1900 people were seated in Westminster. The guide states that it takes over 6 months to prepare Westminster for royal crowning ceremonies, where over 8,000 can be seated, by building temporary extra floors all around this huge church. The first documented coronation in this church is that of William the Conqueror in 1066.

I must admit I did not see the wedding, all busy with my American life of medicine and family, but now I almost think 'How could I have missed it?' This is an event that happens at most every generation. The last royal wedding was at St Paul in 1981, when Charles the Prince of Wales and Diana Spencer got unhappily married. The previous royal wedding at Westminster Abbey was back on 20 November 1947, when Elisabeth II married Prince Philip, made the Duke of Wellington.

I think back, and if we had had a royal private tour guide things would not have been as wonderful and on-time, fitting everything in, as they were. I thank the one above us again.

We then head back to our apartment one last time, close the luggage quickly, and board the tube together. At Piccadilly Circus stop, I have to say bye, sadly, to my heroic fellow journeymen, Paola, Andrea, and Pietro. I kiss Paola on the lips (twice at different times), Pietro once on the cheek, and, since I know he does not like public (or private) displays of affection, I shake Andrea's hand as a goodbye. They have been extraordinary companions. I will continue to think about them often for the rest of this U.K. trip.

I continue on the subway towards the Royal College of Obstetricians and Gynecologists headquarters, located near the tube station of Baker Street, three stops after Piccadilly. I was told it is only a 7-8 minute walk to get to the Royal College. As I'm carrying a large suitcase and a carry-on, I want to make sure I get there as quickly as possible.

I ask for directions a nice station guard, who points me to the right exit. Arrived at Regent Park, a kind taxi driver tells me that Sussex Place must be inside the Park, and I should go back 30 feet to the other street. As I arrive at Sussex Place, a 25-year-old young oxford-looking handsome student with a smile tells me the Royal

College of Obstetricians and Gynecologists (RCOG) is a few yards ahead, continuing on the Outer Circle.

At the RCOG headquarters, as I approach the main reception desk, the pretty Englishwoman is already smiling. 'You must be Professor Berghella,' she says, and my name never sounded better in her British accent. A couple of drops of sweats run down my forehead from logging around my baggage, but I try to look as professional as she made me sound.

She says, caringly: 'Can I take your luggage?' I wish life continues like this forever! A big gentleman appears after 15 seconds, and takes my larger suitcase, which they'll store for me until my return the next day, Wednesday. I head off back to the tube station, then train station, and eventually Liverpool.

I'm so lucky again at the train station. I had booked online in the US a 30-pounds cheap ticket to Liverpool via Crewe, where I would have needed to change. When I had reserved it, I had seen a 90-pound direct ticket just after 3pm, but bought the cheaper 30-pound ticket without realizing I had to change trains.

As I arrive a bit early at London Euston station, I ask the friendly black ticket agent for help converting my paper printout to a real train ticket to Liverpool. She tells me I could take the 14:07 train, direct to Liverpool, for no extra money! Which I immediately do, under her supervision.

I walk to Station #15, and see the long line slowly moving already. So, hungry, I grab on the side of the station's entrance a one-foot-long panino with prosciutto and cheese, and am fast enough to catch the end of the line. So I get in, and the train leaves, are you surprised, exactly at 14:07, on time, as is life in England, which invented the exact time at Greenwich.

Within a minute of the train moving, the captain announces on loud speaker that this is 'the Pendolino service to Liverpool.' In Italy they probably call the frequent connections between Rome and Milan 'Express' service. Here it's more trendy to say 'Pendolino,' which in Italian means something like 'commuter.' I am always amazed at how much fashion affects everything, even the names of trains. I do know that 'the grass is always greener on the other side,' and foreign 'mania' and the gusto of the exotic is something that each of us humans has a bit.

From the train windows I admire the beautiful, mostly sunny day. I'm also reminded that, as my sister Anna always says, 'the weather is changeable in England.' Stormy clouds seem to appear often suddenly on the sky. Under them, I see a very rural landscape, with cows, and green pastures.

I'm clearly in a working class train to Liverpool station, called Liverpool Lime. I study the few people on it. Close to my seat there is a little girl whose mother talks constantly to, very caringly. The kid must be 6 or 7 years old, and has red long hair. I think, jokingly, that she must be related to Pippi Longstockings.

As I arrive in Liverpool, early, I'm a bit lost. While I have a map of the city, it takes me a couple of minutes to realize where is north and where is south. Off the station, I head towards Mount Pleasant Road, and the hotel. I ask directions to everyone in the 0.6miles walk. They are all nice.

This situation reminds me a bit of when in Birmingham, about 32 years ago, I got lost in a suburb and could not even ask directions for where I was going. I did not know the name of the college I was at, and did not know the word 'lake' (which was the only detail of the college I could remember, that it was near a lake). So, to explain the location to astonished passers-by, I mimicked with my hands together a container-like structure, and said 'water,' pointing with my face to the bottom of the 'sac' made by my hands. So much time has passed; I'm almost a different person.

I stroll down the road making sure I examine every detail in front of my eyes. People seem to be squinting at the sun. I guess that maybe they are not used to the late October sun, peaking trough the fast-moving clouds, already low on the horizon. I imagine Liverpool as a blue-collar city, with real people working hard to make ends meet under cloudy skies and little light for much of the year.

The red head at the check-in of the Feathers Hotel is friendly, with a big smile, and makes the place. You can have the best-looking, most luxurious hotel, but your personnel are most important to make you feel welcome.

To my surprise, to get to the room, on the 3rd floor, I have to walk-up narrow and steep stairs, as there is no elevator. The room, while on the top floor, is tiny, barely enough to accommodate a twin-size bed. I can hardly fit in the bathroom, with a windowsill the only minuscule surface on which to put my beauty case. This room, more than anything else, makes me finally understand why four boys in the early 1960's were so eager to sing their way out of Liverpool.

Even if I wanted to, I could not really stay in the room, too depressive. I step out and walk around. The sun is again shining. I see a very new church, brick buildings, and people dressed simply. It's almost 5pm, and as the winter sun is setting, everything gets painted with darker colors. I decide to call my colleague Zarko Alfirevich, to see if I can meet him soon.

To my delight, he answers the phone right away. Once I tell him where I am, by looking at the names of the streets at the corner I'm at, Zarko tells me that I can just walk less than a kilometer to his hospital, Liverpool Women's Hospital. While I head towards this famous institution, I ask several times a middle-aged gentle local woman walking in my same direction if I'm on the right roads.

Liverpool Women's Hospital is a nice building constructed in 1995 on Crown Street. A few women are smoking outside the main entrance. I hope they are not pregnant. A nurse is sitting with them – rebels are everywhere.

Zarko meets me at the entrance. I've known him for many years. He is a well-respected researcher in pregnancy matters. He is also now Co-Chair of the Cochrane Pregnancy Unit. To my delight, we walk right to the 'world' headquarters of the Cochrane Pregnancy and Childbirth Group.

I love the Cochrane. What is it? The Cochrane Library is a collection of medical databases. At its core is the collection of Cochrane Reviews, a series of systematic reviews and meta-analyses which summarize and interpret the results of randomized controlled trials (RCTs). RCTs are the best studies in medicine, and their summary are therefore of paramount importance to inform the physician and other health care workers on what is best to do for different clinical care scenarios.

Archie Cochrane was born in Scotland, and studied at University College Hospital, in London. He was specialized in diseases of the lung, in particular tuberculosis. His experiences during the Spanish Civil War, and later during World War II, led him to believe that much of medicine did not have sufficient evidence to justify its use. He said, "I knew that there was no real evidence that anything we had to offer had any effect on tuberculosis, and I was afraid that I shortened the lives of some of my friends by unnecessary intervention." As a result, he spent his career urging the medical community to adopt the scientific method. His studies pioneered the use of RCTs.

I have written now several Cochrane Reviews myself, have corrected a couple of dozens as Associate Editor, and am an avid reader and user of them. The two medical textbooks I edited on Obstetric Evidence Based Guidelines and Maternal Fetal Evidence Based Guidelines, now in their second edition, refer to all the 400-plus Cochrane Reviews related to pregnancy.

I take a picture of Zarko in front of the Cochrane entrance. I also get introduced to Jim Neilson, the Co-Chair of the Cochrane Group. The plan is for us to spend some time together the next morning; tonight Jim still has some clinical and paper work to attend to.

Zarko leads me then in a wonderful tour of the whole ob-gyn unit. They do over 8,000 deliveries at LGH, of which 2,000 in a midwife-led unit. Zarko, still less diplomatic than most British, tells me that the U.K., to him, is a 'communist country,' with much help for the ones in need, and not many privileges for the well-offs.

He reveals to me that even the wife of Steve Gerrard, the cherished captain of the Liverpool football team (the 'reds'), who is being induced on November 3, will deliver with midwives. Even the wife of Fernando Torres, the former center forward, who also received ultrasounds by Zarko, was eventually delivered by a midwife. There is no consultant doctor on call in-house at night, just midwives, junior registrars, and one senior registrar. But Zarko admits that they are changing to an in-house system soon.

Zarko and I have dinner at a Chinese restaurant. He explains to me that there is no typical food here. In fact, in a recent survey, people in Scotland selected curry as the Scotland national food! The Chinese food is excellent, we eat like kings, and Zarko pays only 24 pounds in total.

From our seats, there is a nice view of Liverpool, and the river Mersey. Liverpool was at some point the second largest city in the British Empire, due to its large port, and money from the slave trade especially, according to Zarko. In the early 19th century, 40% of the world's trade passed through Liverpool's docks.

We are on 'Mersey side', which is the east side of the river towards inland. The area between the two Liverpool rivers, the Mersey and the Dez, has both the worst area of Liverpool, but also the best area, where Zarko, Jim and the other doctors live. Across the river Dez is Wales, as they say, 'another country.' Therese Doswell, one of the others who work at the Cochrane, lives there. Driving me back to the hotel, Zarko tells me of his background, Serbian, his Serbian wife, and his family. He is clearly happy here in Liverpool, and has had much success.

While the jet lag I think it's already gone, it takes me a while to fall asleep. I read all my new books bought at Westminster Abbey on the royal succession lines and the British Kings and Queens in the last 1,000 or so years. I'm just fascinated by history. When I wake up during the night for my not-so-unusual urinary trip to the bathroom, I have trouble falling back asleep, given the drip from the heating unit.

October 26, Wednesday

My plan for this morning is to join Jim Neilson, the Co-Chair of the Pregnancy and Childbirth branch of the Cochrane Library, at Liverpool Women's Hospital. I have a quick breakfast, and then meet Jim in the lobby of the hotel at 8am, right on time, as planned.

Jim Neilson is Scottish. I think right away of Ferguson, Manchester United soccer mythical coach, but Ferguson's accent is thicker, at least on TV. Jim is tall, thin, distinguished. He is married. His only daughter just qualified as a doctor, and perhaps will be an emergency department specialist, or an anesthesiologist. I think Jim is also proud of the fact that she is training in Glasgow, back in Scotland, where both him and his wife are from.

While Zarko drove a BMW, Jim drives a VW, and this consideration is already a simple description of the two men. Jim is much understated, modest, and discreet. I myself drive a BMW, but admire major scientists like Jim who wear their fame without being at all ostentatious. I like his easiness, his serenity.

We seat down for an hour in his office. But we could talk for a lot longer. It's amazing how doing similar work, even thousands of miles apart, can bring people so close. It's like we have always known each other. Our work, his for over 30 years, mine for almost 20, has covered similar topics, all related to pregnancy, and we are certainly interested in the same goal, improving the health of mothers and their babies.

From 9:05am or so, in the Cochrane office, I talk to Therese Dowswell, in charge of the special project of updating priority reviews, about fifty in about three years. Later Lynn Hampson also arrives. She is in charge of all the searches. A monster job: over 16,000 randomized controlled trials (RCTs) related to pregnancy have been printed, categorized and stored. Over 12,000 of them are saved as PDFs. This is the job of a part-time employee called Ann, who is not here today.

I think that Lynn has an extremely important job. The whole world should have access to this massive classification of precious knowledge. Lynn also looks at journals tables of contents for potential articles, which then she saves in her computer, adding it to the large database. She finds at least 20 new good RCTs on pregnancy-related matters to possibly include every week, mostly trough PubMed and EMBASE, but also trough Central, which are all websites which list medical manuscripts. Then she fits them in the right category.

Both Therese and Lynn are pleasant and friendly. The more I talk to them, the more I grasp the enormity of their tasks. I do feel a bit of an intruder, talking time away from their precious work. I've written or co-written now almost ten Cochrane Reviews, and edited almost twice as many. I do hope that I'll be able to continue to contribute to this vital effort, which should be better known, funded, and utilized worldwide.

I have lunch with Jim. He is done with his clinic. The night before he had taken call from home, and was therefore responsible for all deliveries at the hospital. Clearly he continues to have a busy clinical schedule. I admire the fact that such an illustrious researcher, even if into his 60's, continues to have direct interactions with patients. To me this is the key to be able to come up constantly with new ideas and be able to contribute important advances in clinical management.

As planned, after lunch I'm headed to the Liverpool train station, and then back to London. The taxi driver is talkative. Liverpool has a lot of Irish immigrants, he explains. It makes sense, since this is the biggest port on the Irish Sea that separates the two biggest British Isles. He is pissed that the Irish Club, which is close to the Feathers' Hotel where I had stayed, was closed for renovations years ago, and never reopened. I do not have the guts to ask if he is of Irish descent, but his demeanor tells me he is.

On the train, the clouds I see from the windows are so low I can almost touch them. I'm getting used to this: 'the weather is indeed changeable in England.' The sun from the west hits me, warms me up, and makes me groggy. I relax and doze off, may be five minutes. I've learned recently that napping is healthy, if one feels the need to. So, as is in my demeanor, I follow the scientific advice. When I wake up, I notice through the window a large nuclear plant.

It seems like I have made sure that every minute of this United Kingdom trip is organized so to get the most out of it. While the reason to be here was the Royal College of Obstetrics and Gynecology (RCOG) meeting on Friday, I had also arranged to attend a British Journal of Obstetrics and Gynecology (BJOG) meeting on Thursday. But my professional connections with this country are even more.

Another very important one is with Informa Healthcare, a medical publishing company. Since 2005, I've been collaborating with them on several projects. The most important, and for me one of my greatest personal professional achievements, is the publication of the two medical textbooks I mentioned previously: Maternal Fetal Evidence Based Guidelines, and Obstetric Evidence Based Guidelines. Informa is the publishing house for these books, and I'm the editor.

Published first in 2007, these books have sold thousands of copied all over the world, about 55% in the United States, but also 45% in the rest, including all continents. They have been translated, even in Turkish. While a ton of work, the satisfaction that this project has given me is hard to understate. Given their success, a second edition has been commissioned, and, together with dozens of wonderful collaborators, I have completed editing the 87 chapters and almost 800 pages.

So I'm looking forward to meet Robert Peden face-to-face in London. He is the publisher at Informa, and has overlooked the production of both first and second editions of my evidence-based books. We have probably exchanged over one hundred emails just in 2011, and it's nice to finally have some time to speak directly.

He had proposed to meet at St Pancras, a tube station close to my Liverpool-London train arrival at Euston Station. So, pushing my light, wheeled, carry-on bag, I walk the short distance, enjoying the crowded streets of London around 5pm. As I stroll past a bus stop, I noticed a young brunette, with black hair and big light bleu eyes, exchanging my stare, seemingly interested.

I arrive perhaps two minutes after our scheduled time of 5pm, and find the meeting place, under a big large statue of two commuters, a young boy and a young girl, kissing. The statue is so large, made of very dark metal, that it reminds me of some work from the Mussolini era. As soon as my eyes come down to the ground from scrutinizing the sculpture, I see Robert Peden.

Robert is as usual well-dressed, elegant. He is tall, almost as me, thin, neat. We seat down at one of the bars. He is gentle and calm. The waitress serves me the smallest bagels I've ever seen, with some cream cheese, and tasty lox (smoked salmon). I was hoping in a few more calories. I also drink a juice. Robert and I talk relaxingly for over one hour.

Given that our common project, the second editions of the two medical textbooks, is going well, we have time to also talk about personal life, and several other non-professional topics. He tells me about his background, his history. I imagine his apartment sparkles, in south London. He does worry about his job. As he has lasted so long, he must be good, and bringing profits to Informa.

I hop back on two different tube lines, to get to my destination for the night. On the way, I buy myself a long prosciutto and cheese sandwich, and an apple. I check in at the Royal College of Obstetrics and Gynecology (RCOG) headquarters at 7:30pm or so. The exact address is 27 Sussex Place, Regents Park, NW1 4RG London. The name of the 'hotel' inside the RCOG, basically a few royal rooms, is The Domus. I hold reservation #1552. Not too many have had the privilege of being hosted here.

My room, 303, is next to the Presidential suite. It is a beautiful stylish room, quiet and royal. There is mahogany color furniture, two bathrooms, one with bath, another one with a huge shower. I have ample time tonight, in splendid peaceful surroundings, for the first time, to take it easy. I empty my luggage, and hang my bleu jacket and white shirts. Tomorrow and the next day, I'll be using them again.

I could call several of my friends, such as Olivier, Andrea, Raffaella, even Simona Cicero, but I decide instead to relax. I imagine them all immersed in their busy London lives, and do not want to disturb. For me, I admit that I've already packed enough activities so far in this wonderful trip.

So I settle in, and decide to spend the rest of the night at 303 RCOG Domus, my royal room. Unfortunately, the flat screen TV blocks the soccer matches, tonight they are showing both Carling Cup games and Serie A games. Sigh. I instead have a great time watching Mister Bean. I have lots of hardy British carefree laughs, and feel this is most appropriate given where I'm geographically located.

October 27, Thursday

Today is the day of my British Journal of Obstetrics and Gynecology (BJOG) Editorial meeting, to be held, according to the schedule I was given months ago by Elisabeth Hay and Emily Jesper, at 10:30am-16:30pm, right here at the RCOG headquarters.

I take a great shower. The shower room is huge. One walks in it as the whole room is just for showering, with a grey granite floor. Once I step out of the room, the RCOG headquarters seem so quiet. The place is all for myself. There are RCOG symbols everywhere, on the carpets, on the walls.

On the 2nd floor, just one floor below me, as I had read, there is the breakfast room. I easily find the signs for it. The 'Royal' Guests dining room is indeed regal, old-looking, graceful. I'm the only one there. As everywhere else in the building, huge painted portraits hang from the tall walls.

I have a wonderful breakfast, with private service. The large table seats about eight, but the two waitresses are there just for me. Coffee? Tea? Toast? They bring me in 30 seconds four pieces of toasted bread. I have cereal, toast, and peaches in syrup. I do spend a few minutes looking at my surroundings, which include a large living room, with big formal sofas. They look very comfortable. I imagine how peaceful it would be to open an old classic book and read a few hours in silence here. I am attracted by the portraits of William Blair-Bell, the founder of the RCOG, and I read a bit of his story.

I visit the whole place, each floor. I see the museum pieces, including some of the earliest forceps (invented here in England) ever used. I enjoy the famous phrases written on the walls, including this one: 'Anyone entering a hospital was exposed to more chance of death than was an English soldier at Waterloo,' by Sir James Simpson. There are many lecture rooms, pharmaceutical-companies-sponsored glass rooms, long corridors.

I look for the rooms where my meetings will be. The BJOG editorial meetings, according to my schedule, which I have saved from months ago, are supposed to happen in the Wyeth Room. I find it on the Ground floor, left from the entrance, down a hallway. The sign says Wyethroom, may be to disguise the apparent sponsorship.

I also visit the library. I'm a huge fan of books, and I look at each one, to get an idea what the RCOG and the British in general read here. As I'm looking, I do find my Maternal Fetal Evidence Based Guidelines book, and I'm elated!

In the bookstore, they are actually selling all the three medical books I've published so far, the Maternal Fetal Evidence Based Guidelines book, the Obstetric Evidence Based Guidelines book, and the Preterm birth: Prevention and Management book, this last one in print with Wiley-Blackwell Publishing. Sure, there is some vanity into looking for one's own books, but it is so rewarding to see so much hard work getting recognized, and utilized. There are many books on ob-gyn, I want to buy at least two or three of them, especially on the history of our specialty, but resist the temptation.

I walk one more floor down, and find a beautiful Lecture Hall. I go and look for rooms L1 and L2, where a program had listed the RCOG Early Cerclage meeting to be (the one I'm supposed to speak at tomorrow, Friday). I find them at the end of a long hallway, and I'm disappointed. The rooms are regular rooms, they only fit 30 or 40 people, on regular chairs, and the projector screen is not that big.

Oh, how much would I rather the RCOG meeting to be in the Lecture Hall! This may well be the opportunity of a lifetime. I do not think about it then, but as I reflect on those thoughts now, it was like for an Orchestra Director to have been invited to London, and to find out that the performance is not at Covent Garden, but at a smaller theater just down the road. Well, nothing I can do about it, I think. A bigger meeting with a larger audience and more famous speakers must be going on in the Lecture Hall. I'll do my best with the opportunity I've been given.

I head back to my room. My laptop computer is not working!! Preparation is everything in life, but I have other ways to be ready. I have different manila folders for each of my four professional events, Cochrane in Liverpool, Informa publisher, BJOG meeting, and RCOG conference. I review briefly and take with me my BJOG notes, after reviewing also briefly my printed RCOG slides for tomorrow, Friday. I make my way down at 10:10am, ahead of the time for the BJOG meeting, set in my emails from Jessica and Kim for 10:30am in the Wyeth room.

As I walk in the Wyeth room though, there are two people already there at 10:18am, and they seem to have nothing to do with BJOG. I wait a bit outside the corridor that one has to take to get to this room, hoping to see some BJOG staff go by, hopefully the Editor-in-chief, Phil Steer. But no luck. So I walk again in the Wyeth room, and inquire. Indeed there is no BJOG meeting there at 10:30am, the man and woman tell me, with a tiny bit of annoyance at my barging in this second time.

So I go to the entrance desk of the RCOG, where a nice, very British looking, black hair and blue eyes assistant (which I begin to know well from all the questions I ask her all the time) tells me that indeed the room is another one. I go then down the stairs, a floor below, and finally, through glass walls, see about a dozen people around a table, with Phil Steer easily recognizable among them.

As I walk in, a feel a bit embarrassed as I think I might be a bit late, since an electronic billboard I just saw announced the BJOG Editorial meeting for 10am. Nobody told me. As I enter the large conference room, Phil in front of everyone else says an affectionate hello of welcome to me, and also that the meeting has not started yet. Emily and Lizzy greet me warmly, and tell me to go seat next to Phil. An honor. Later I'll realize that the computer I'm assigned does not connect to the internet reliably, and I would have to ask for IT help, eventually providing another laptop. Not such a great seat after all.

John Thorp is the only other US Editor to attend this editorial meeting, and he'll be two hours late, for no particular reason that he announces. So my showing up exactly at 10:30am before the meeting started looks great. The little things we all worry about.

The meeting goes well. George Macones, another maternal-fetal medicine US specialist who trained two years before me at Thomas Jefferson University in Philadelphia, is the one who told me to make sure to actively participate in meetings. I also know that opening one's mouth just to talk without a good point to contribute makes one self's only look foolish, revealing ineptitude that could have been better stayed hidden.

So I probably make brief and topical interventions about seven or so times during the almost four-hour meeting, interrupted by a quick sandwich lunch. My idea of giving the nickname 'blue journal' to BJOG is well-liked. Phil seems to be in favor of a 'Cochrane corner' in BJOG, and gives me contacts at Wiley-Blackwell to get it done.

After the meeting is over, I sneak out of the RCOG headquarters to go to the Geek Squad electronics store to fix my laptop. In Boston, a year and a half ago, it had taken only a few minutes to fix the same issue. In my head, I hope that it will be the same deal now. I call to confirm they are still there and open, but get no one to pick up my call. I decide to go anyway.

They are located about two tube stops from me, but I would have to change, so I decide to walk. Even in this early London afternoon, around 3pm, the sidewalks are at times so full of people it's hard to get through. I do find the Geek Squad store following my iPhone map. There is a line, but eventually I get to talk with a 'geek.' I hope a good one.

Initially he does not think this is fixable. I struggle to remember how they resolved the same issue before in Boston, but I cannot. They are not able to assess the US database for Geek

Squad here in London. He brings the computer back to the lab. I do hope now someone else will figure it out.

After about five interminable minutes, he comes back with a smile. Some keys on the keyboard are not working properly. So he hooks up the laptop to another external keyboard, and, voila', he turns on the laptop! As it happened in Boston, here again the Geek Squad friendly staff does not charge me, and insures me that, as long as I keep the laptop on, this should not happen again. I walk quickly back to my RCOG Domus room, to keep the laptop alive by plugging it into the electrical power cord.

The Editor-in-Chief had asked me to join other BJOG Editors for a meal that night, but at least six months ago Roy Farquharson had invited me also to dinner. He is the organizer of the RCOG scientific meeting I am to attend the next day, Friday. To my delight, my great friend Sean Daly is also going to be there. I quickly clean up again into jacket and tie, and step out to yet another tube ride.

We are to have dinner at the Caledonian club, at 9 Halkin Street, London, SW1X7DR, in Belgravia, near Hyde Park Corner and Buckingham Palace Gardens. As I walk to the entrance, a black taxi cab arrives, and… Sean Daly steps out of it. Our smiles are sincere as we give each other a big hug. I really, really admire Sean, a wonderful person, complete not only as a smart, dedicated, and successful medical professional, but also as a loyal husband and a caring father of four.

Roy Farquharson is waiting for us sipping drinks on a comfortable couch, and greets us warmly. We are all set for our plan for 7:30 drinks, and 8pm dinner. Originally founded in 1891 as a proprietary club, The Caledonian Club as it is today was formed in 1917 under the energetic leadership of the Marquis of Tullibardine. He made it the representative national club and headquarters for Scotsmen in London. Roy, a long-time member of the club, clearly loves this enclave just for Scottish people, men and women.

While the exterior is simple, the interior is grand. The Club occupies five floors and comprises the Members' Dining Room, Drawing Room, "Smoking" Room and Library, together with five meeting and private dining rooms, with capacity up to 250. Bedroom accommodations are situated on the two upper floors. Roy is staying here, as he always does when he's here in London from his home in Liverpool. Alan Cameron, another famous Scottish ob-gyn, from Glasgow, also to talk at the conference the next day, joins us.

As usual, I first ask Roy what is the food most typical to eat there, and then I order it. The appetizer is some kind of tuber, a fancy potato pure', called haggis, which is to be covered with malt Scotch whisky (wee dram). A wee dram, or 'small spirits', is what Scottish people call 'their favorite drink.' The main course is tender beef, a large portion, with claret, which is a dark red wine from Bordeaux, very good. My friends drink more alcohol than I could safely knock back. The conversation is lively, and, while I'm the only one from the west side of the Atlantic, or also from the south side of the English Channel, they make me feel quite at home.

Given that the next day all of us need to speak, coherently, at the RCOG conference, we spend only a few minutes relaxing in the couches in the library after dinner. Sean helps me decline Roy offer for some more malt-based drinks, and we split, me back to my royal apartment at RCOG.

October 28, Friday

I sleep well. I'm used now to give talks at international events, as I must have given hundreds of them, in four continents, and overall must have given thousands, literally thousands of public talks on medical topics. Today, the topic of the whole conference is cerclage, and I know I master this subject.

As I walk downstairs, this time I ask where exactly the 'cerclage' RCOG conference is. To my delight, the kind official walks me to the beautiful Lecture Hall, the one I dreamed about! I'm a very happy guy now! I load my slides, as usual well ahead of time, and I know my preparations now have been perfect and complete.

In the RCOG 'Early pregnancy cerclage', I have a big part of the morning to fill, with a 10-10:30am 'Evidence and Utility of screening the cervix' lecture, followed by a 11:20-12:10am 'Clinical applications of cervical length measurements' second lecture. Each talk is followed by a scheduled question session.

My lectures go well. One major confirmation of interest is after the lecture, i.e. the questions I get. For both, I get lots of excellent queries. I'm on time for the first talk, as I speak for 30 minutes, with 20 minutes of questions. The moderators, Sean and Roy, cannot stop the audience for throwing several interesting inquiries at me.

I'm probably a bit too brief for the second lecture, where I'm supposed to talk for 50 minutes, but I forget at what time I've started, and can't figure out when I should finish. So I probably finish ten minutes too soon, as usual breezing excitedly through my other 70 slides. The questions though take us all the way to 12:30am, exactly as scheduled.

There are again at least a dozen, smart, good questions, clearly from active clinicians who deal with the issues I talk about all the time. One person, 'Donald', apparently a private physician in London, states that one large study, the largest ever on cerclage, was 'rubbish', tearing it apart. As the study was by the RCOG, is now about 20 years old, and still determines care and guidelines, I feel this is a bit of an exaggeration. No study is perfect. I have the guts to joke in my reply saying: 'I'm glad you do not feel too strongly about it.' I get a polite laugh from the audience.

Later, during the break, Donald approaches me and is friendly, as he was able to take the remark in the gentle and humorous manner in which it was meant. Throughout the day, at least ten eager obstetricians or midwives from the audience seek my personal one-on-one attention for questions. A couple of them move me, as they say they read everything I publish, as it is (their term) 'excellent', 'must-read.'

When Andrew Shennan presents in the afternoon, I have a moment of pure joy inside. He is a renowned professor at King's College, and practices at the famous Thomas and Guy's Hospital, near the apartment we stayed with my family earlier in the week. He is one of the gurus in preterm birth and on cerclage here in the United Kingdom, a fact I did not know well. I had heard his name, and read a few of his studies, but was pleasantly surprised as he was introduced by Roy with much fanfare.

In his talk, he reviews the just published (May 2011) RCOG 'Green Top' Guidelines on Cerclage. In each slides, he goes through one or two of the statements for clinical advice. Each statement is given a 'grade', A for statement with the best evidence, D for a statement with poorest evidence, and also RCOG general recommendation for statements purely based on good clinical common sense.

I'm delighted: I agree with each statement. A lot of the evidence on which these recommendations are based comes from papers I've written. The beauty is he has not even listened to my two hours of talking, as he was busy in his clinic in the morning.

There is only one level A evidence statement: that women with singleton gestations, prior preterm birth, and a short cervical length of less than 25 mm should be recommended cervical cerclage. Yeah!! This is the aspect of cerclage I've researched the most. There are randomized studies on this topic, and I'm first author on one, and author on another one (the largest and most recent). I've also written two meta-analyses (summary studies) about this issue, and plenty of chapters and other articles.

I feel years of hard work have paid off. Someone who does not even know me personally, has never met me before, Prof Andrew Shennan, on the other side of the Atlantic, working completely independently from me or any of my collaborators, has trusted the goodness of our work, and now recommends on a national level to implement what we have helped discover. This is a lifetime achievement.

On every slide he keeps on showing recommendations which I could have written. Perhaps the best part is that my name is not on any slides, as he does not mention references. So I can celebrate this achievement quietly in the comfort of my chair, gleaming. And when statements are purposely vague because the data in the literature is not yet clear regarding safety and effectiveness of the intervention, Andy mentions that he'd be 'curious to know what Professor Berghella thinks.' Wow.

When his question and answer session comes, I cannot resist from being the first to publicly congratulate him. My accent is much different than his perfect British one. So I'm not sure he and others understand when I say that 'I was going imaginary flips of joy in my chair during most of your talk.' The expression comes from that Vincenzo in me that can never stop being a happy little kid.

After the conference, Roy insists on taking four of us speakers to the pub just behind the RCOG headquarters. He says 'it's tradition.' Much of life is tradition to him, which is great, and reminds me a bit of my dad. Of course, even at 4-5pm, the pub is crowded. After all, it's Friday afternoon.

I order whatever beer they have ordered, but I'm the only one not to finish it. This early in the afternoon a pint of beer would ruin the rest of my day, as I'd have a useless brain for at least 3-4 hours, and then also get a headache. I am extremely thankful to Roy and

Sean, as I have had a terrific time. I have written this little book of memories also to show them my gratitude.

Everyone else has a plane or a train to catch. I can retrieve to the quietness of my RCOG room, where jacket and tie finally come off, and can go to rest. Now I have the remainder of the evening free, either to relax and enjoy being by myself, or to organize with whomever I want. I know I'm not that good to be in solitude.

Simona Cicero is an obstetrician originally from Puglia, Italy, who became well-known while working in London with perhaps the most famous European pregnancy researcher, Professor Kipros Nicolaides. She published a lot around the time she was with him.

I will never forget, at one of the Society for Maternal-Fetal Medicine meetings years ago in the United States, when an Irish researcher attacked some of her studies. While he was rude and inappropriate, she, from the audience, replied in a professional manner, despite being probably less than 30 years old, and in front of an international audience in a foreign land.

I've been impressed with her publications. Years ago, when I knew she was in the US for talks, I invited her to swing by Philadelphia. She gave a good talk at Grand Rounds, and she came for dinner at our house. Simona had emailed me a few weeks back regarding an invitation to dinner at her house. I had understood that she was coming to the RCOG conference, and that then we would go to her house. She is married now, with two young kids.

So, when I do not see her at the meeting, I ask Jessica, one of the assistants at RCOG, if she had signed up. In fact, I even find Simona's name in my contacts, and send her an email, as I do not have her cell. Simona answers me back within 30 minutes. She profusely apologizes, saying that she has had ten terrible days, working hard and also busy with sick kids at home, etc. She is on call tonight, and there is really no chance to meet.

When we later talk on the phone, around 7:30pm, after she has done an emergency cesarean in her role as Senior Registrar, she clarifies that in fact she had told me by email months ago she was going to be on call tonight, and that dinner was possible on any other day. Well, misunderstanding there, no problem.

I feel Simona looks up to me a bit, but more as a good guy who is happily married and has made it by himself both professionally and personally, representing therefore an example to follow, then as an international obstetric 'star.' That makes me even happier, more proud. I am impressed by her work ethic. Efficient, honest people, for the most part, can make it anywhere in the world, especially outside of Italy. The world is getting smaller, and it pays to move where opportunities are.

It's my last night in London. I'm not going to spend it in the room, even if it's tempting. I go out, and walk around. I stroll on Baker Street, Bond Street, and many others. I call Paola, who tells me to call Olivier and Andrea, for company. She knows me well. In fact, nobody knows me better than her.

Strangely, I'm actually enjoying the time alone, a stranger in the busy streets of London. I think 'who knows who I'll meet.' I eye of course every beautiful girl. None is as beautiful as the black thin one I saw in the tube two days ago, or the white black hair blue eyes one I saw while walking from Euston Station to St Pancras to meet Robert Peden.

Olivier does not answer his cell. Andrea does, and he is about to go to a party. I just say hello thanking him for the company on Monday night. So I continue my solitary walk. I am indeed a very social person, and I do not tolerate being just by myself too much. But the evening is fresh, 50 plus degrees, no rain.

I'm very at ease in my favorite and I think fashionable dark and soft blue jeans, and my trademark white and blue stripes shirt and blue sweater, which I think makes me look thinner. I assume a lot of women look at me. May be it's just that I'm tall. I purposely force myself to walk a bit slower than usual, like to relax myself, and, for once, to enjoy just being alive. Everyone else seems to be rushing by.

There are already some youngsters with costumes heading to Halloween parties. Only a lonely short Asian girl, with a large hard suitcase on her back probably containing a musical instrument, seems to walks a bit slower. She has a Pret-A-Manger bag with what I suppose is some food in it. She seems to want to walk right next to me.

Then she gains may be one foot ahead, and stops at the window of a shop, not even lit, and I think looks my way, while pretending to stare closely at something greenish in the shop window. Is she trying to get my attention? I imagine she is heading to a small apartment, by herself, with the small Pret-A-Manger dinner, and would not mind some company. Twenty feet ahead, by coincidence, I take a right while she takes a left.

Dinner in my room is great. I buy myself first, at a Starbucks, an apple fritter (yummy!) and a small ham and cheese sandwich. Later, I also buy at a Pret-A-Manger (they are everywhere) a small bag of mixed nuts and dried fruit, an apple, and a protein bar, so I do not go hungry later before going to bed. Hunger makes it really hard for me to fall asleep.

After dinner, I do 90% of my luggage preparation. I then read for over two hours the books I'd bought at Westminster Abbey regarding the Kings and Queens of England, and also Ireland and Wales and Scotland, depending on the period. The Royal line in the U.K. is really European, in fact probably the most European family around, as the heirs to the throne usually married the firstborn of other royal families such as the French, German, Spanish, and even Russian.

October 29, Saturday

I sleep great. The clothes I had washed the day before are dry, a miracle. A take a beautiful shower, and have a nice quick breakfast. Then I'm off to the Jubilee line, two stops to Green Park, and after seventeen stops to Heathrow. I have to get off at Houslow West, to catch the tube which goes all the way to terminal 5, the international one.

The laptop makes me mad. I upgrade to World Traveller Plus for about 170 extra pounds (I hope Paola does not reprimand me too much) to be able to use the computer on the plane. This old laptop only has about two hours of 'juice,' or autonomy on battery only. On a flight of seven plus hours I would miss many hours during which I can be productive. And if I do not write the story of a trip right away, I miss the opportunity. Once I land, I get into my routine Philadelphia life, with kids to take to places, wife to collaborate at least a bit for household issues, work issues, etc.

I'm told by British Airways personnel that these seats in World Traveler Plus in fact have plugs, and so my 170 pounds is an investment, which I'm glad I can make, even if I do feel a bit guilty about it. Happily, while my computer locks up again, a nice guy in a computer Nokia store in 30 seconds helps me with an external drive to turn the computer on. I hate my 'control-alt-delete,' I guess it's time a buy a new computer, iPAD anyone?

Today is the day of birthdays and anniversaries: Livia Masci my niece (my sister Anna's daughter) is 14, Tonino Testa best man at my wedding is 47, my parents got married on this date in 1962, and I met Paola, the biggest event of my life probably after my birth, in 1993. Wow!!

I can't get Livia, still in school, but when I call her house in Sulmona my mother answers! So I can give her and my dad their happy anniversary. What a successful marriage. I hope they last a lot longer. My mother will forward my best wishes to Livia. I also get Tonino. In fact, his wonderful, smart wife Nicoletta answers his cell phone. They are about to leave for Florence on a mini holiday, given the long weekend with Monday off for All Saints. I'll give Paola an anniversary hug when I arrive.

The BA flight leaves on time at 12:45pm, scheduled to arrive in Philadelphia at 3:35pm. There are no plugs in World Traveler Plus. I politely report this and my story to the stewardess, who calls her supervisor. They apologize, but there is nothing they can do. They take my name and information down, saying I'll be refunded, and given some kind of gift. I never heard again from BA again about this.

I always finish my plate, even on this plane ride, where the chicken with leeks gets a good 'B', probably given my appetite. Finishing the food on my plate is entrenched in me: can I blame my mother? Who knows, perhaps it was my poor ancestors who feared hunger so much that this behavior is now ingrained in me. I always feel that, if I go hungry, I'll get a headache, and won't feel well.

So I live by the conviction that I should eat just a bit more than needed to survive, in case the next meal comes late. I finish everything that is in front of me, voraciously. I often tell myself, to justify frequent large meals, that, being 6'3", my body mass deserves more calories than the average person. The pear dessert gets an A!

Acknowledgements

Paola Luzi, Sean Daly